A PASTORAL PROPHET

Smyth & Helwys Publishing, Inc.
6316 Peake Road
Macon, Georgia 31210-3960
1-800-747-3016
©2017 by William Powell Tuck
All rights reserved.

Library of Congress Cataloging-in-Publication Data

Names: Oates, Wayne E. (Wayne Edward), 1917-1999, author. | Tuck, William
    Powell, 1934- editor.
Title: A pastoral prophet : sermons and prayers of Wayne E. Oates / edited by
    William Powell Tuck.
Description: Macon : Smyth & Helwys, 2017. | Includes bibliographical
    references.
Identifiers: LCCN 2017012257 | ISBN 9781573129558 (pbk. : alk. paper)
Subjects: LCSH: Pastoral psychology--Sermons. | Pastoral psychology--Prayers
    and devotions. | Christianity--Psychology--Sermons. |
    Christianity--Psychology--Prayers and devotions.
Classification: LCC BV4012 .O25 2017 | DDC 252/.061--dc23
LC record available at https://lccn.loc.gov/2017012257

Disclaimer of Liability: With respect to statements of opinion or fact available in this work of nonfiction, Smyth & Helwys Publishing Inc. nor any of its employees, makes any warranty, express or implied, or assumes any legal liability or responsibility for the accuracy or completeness of any information disclosed, or represents that its use would not infringe privately-owned rights.

Advance Praise for *A Pastoral Prophet*

The heart and soul of a gifted spiritual mentor often elude paper and pen, but this compendium of sermons and prayers of Wayne Oates are a faithful and keen reflection of a man who shaped the ministry of many pastors and teachers. Bill Tuck has done us all an enduring favor by capturing the substance of a *rabboni* who blended psychology and religion into messages of eternal insight.

—*Daniel G. Bagby, PhD*
Theodore F. Adams Emeritus Professor of Pastoral Care
Baptist Theological Seminary at Richmond

Every day I have the privilege to sit in the Oates Institute office surrounded by the Wayne Oates Library. Hundreds of volumes addressing subject matter like psychiatry, psychology, ethics, spirituality, theology, biblical studies, medicine, psychology of religion and much more line the shelves. Moreover, there are provocative dissertations written by Wayne's graduate students. Most notable are Bibles used by Oates in his ministry. One can readily see and feel the influence of so many academic and scholarly sources on his work.

William Tuck did a yeoman's task of editing and organizing the sermons and prayers in an engaging manner. I would like to share our gratitude on behalf of the Oates Institute and all who will be touched by this labor of love.

As I read the sermons and prayers in this book, I was amazed, inspired, challenged, and comforted by the exegesis, integration, style, and impact. I couldn't put the book down and was astounded at how contemporary the application of the Bible narrative is for the personal and societal problems we face today. Wayne's extraordinary awareness of the human dilemma and his Holy Spirit-inspired vision of God's and humankind's needed response is uncanny. If you don't want to be challenged and cared for out of the depths of this legendary minister's preaching, then don't start this book. If, on the other hand, you would l like to be rocketed forward into a wonderful spiritual journey, then begin!

—*Rick Underwood, DMin*
Director, Oates Institute, Louisville, Kentucky

Bill Tuck masterfully catches the essence of pastoral care pioneer Wayne Oates's teaching through these sermons and prayers. An illustration in one of Wayne's sermons was of a ten-year-old girl who found her father after he tragically killed himself with a pistol. Wayne spoke of "following this young girl" for four or five years closely, and beautifully describes how he nurtured, pastored, and loved this girl by calling, visiting, or writing regularly to remind her that she was not alone. Wayne Oates walked the talk of his preaching. I know because I was one of the fortunate recipients of his pastoral care like many others in his lifetime. This book reminds us of the foundation of faith that undergirded Wayne's ministry.

—*Malcolm Marler, DMin*
Director of Pastoral Care, UAB Medicine, Birmingham, Alabama
(Former Associate Pastor for Pastoral Care with Bill Tuck as senior pastor at St. Matthews Baptist Church, and a former Chaplain Resident and colleague of Wayne Oates)

Read these sermons and prayers and look directly into the heart of Wayne Oates. He was a consummate counselor, theologian, and writer, but first of all he was a pastor. His identity—his very heart—was that of a pastor to people in the midst of life's struggles. No struggle was foreign to him: depression, divorce, suicide, grief: he shied away from nothing. He gave voice to our deepest hurts, then followed with words we long to hear: you are not alone.

—*Kay Shurden, EdD*
Associate Professor Emeritus, Clinical Education,
Mercer University School of Medicine, Macon, Georgia

A Pastoral Prophet

Sermons and Prayers of Wayne E. Oates

WILLIAM POWELL TUCK, EDITOR

Also by William Powell Tuck

The Way for All Seasons: Reflections on the Beatitudes for the 21st Century
Facing Grief and Death: Living with Dying
The Struggle for Meaning (editor)
Knowing God: Religious Knowledge in the Theology of John Baillie
Our Baptist Tradition
Ministry: An Ecumenical Challenge (editor)
Getting Past the Pain
A Glorious Vision
The Bible as Our Guide for Spiritual Growth (editor)
Authentic Evangelism
The Lord's Prayer Today
The Way for All Seasons
Through the Eyes of a Child
Christmas Is for the Young . . . Whatever Their Age
Love as a Way of Living
The Compelling Faces of Jesus
The Left Behind Fantasy
The Ten Commandments: Their Meaning Today
Facing Life's Ups and Downs
The Church in Today's World
The Church under the Cross
Modern Shapers of Baptist Thought in America
The Journey to the Undiscovered Country: What's beyond Death?
A Pastor Preaching: Toward a Theology of the Proclaimed Word
The Pulpit Ministry of the Pastors of River Road Church, Baptist (editor)
The Last Words from the Cross
Overcoming Sermon Block: The Preacher's Workshop
Holidays, Holy Days, and Special Days
A Revolutionary Gospel: Salvation in the Theology of Walter Rauschenbusch
A Positive Word for Christian Lamenting: Funeral Homilies
The Forgotten Beatitude: Worshiping through Stewardship
Star Thrower: A Pastor's Handbook

With appreciation
for
Wayne E. Oates,
who influenced me
and many others
through his
teaching, writing, preaching,
and personal support

Acknowledgments

With appreciation to Smith Reynolds Library Special Collections & Archives at Wake Forest University, Winston-Salem, North Carolina, for permission to use several of Wayne Oates's sermons and prayers: "How Can I Know the Will of God?," "Despair: A Lesson of the Soul," "The Wrath of God and the Destiny of Man," "The Christian Peace in Time of War," "Prayer for Peace," "Guiding Lights for Caring Pastors," and "Remembering and Being Leaders."

With appreciation to Charles E. Oates, MD, for permission to use pictures of Wayne Oates.

With appreciation to the Center for Baptist Heritage & Studies for permission to use some material in the chapter "Wayne Oates: Pastoral Prophet" in *Modern Shapers of Baptist Thought in America*, edited by William Powell Tuck (Richmond, VA: Center for Baptist Heritage & Studies, 2012).

Wayne E. Oates

Contents

Foreword by G. Wade Rowatt	xiii
Preface	xv
Introduction: Wayne E. Oates as a Preacher	1

Part I: Sermons — 5
1. The Need for Roots — 7
2. What Christ Means to Me — 13
3. The Face of Jesus Christ — 19
4. The Providence of God and Our Temptations — 23
5. The Better Way: The Ethic of Wholeness — 29
6. The Ministry of Encouragement — 35
7. The Church: A Many-splendored Fellowship — 41
8. The Community of Faith, Comfort, and Ministry — 47
9. What Do You Say to Yourself? — 53
10. Flying, Running, Walking — 57
11. The Daily Providence of God — 63
12. The Struggle for Maturity — 67
13. How Can We Know the Will of God? — 75
14. Guiding Lights for the Caring Pastor — 79
15. Remembering and Being Leaders — 85
16. Security in Conflict — 93
17. Despair: A Disease of the Soul — 97
18. The Wrath of God and the Destiny of Man — 103

Part II: Prayers — 111
   Introduction — 113
   Selected Prayers — 115
      Crises as "End Situations" — 115
      Crises as "Leaps of Faith" vs. "Shrinking Back" — 115

Crises as Emergencies or Threats to Survival	116
Crisis Accumulation as Stress	116
Stress Management and Pastoral Care	117
A Pastoral Interpretation of Stress and Stress Management	117
Pastoral Initiative and Crisis Intervention	118
The Life Support System and Crisis Management	118
The Crises of Grief and Separation	119
The Crises Surrounding Birth	120
The Crises of Physical Illness and Trauma	120
The Crisis of Marital Conflict	121
The Crisis of Divorce	122
The Crisis of Depression	122
The Crisis of Suicide	123
The Crisis of Psychotic Breaks with Reality	123
The Crises of Educational Mobility and Alienation	124
The Crises of Religious Alienation: Social and Spiritual	124
For a Person Who Is Dying	125
Prayer of Dedication for Families	125
Closing Prayers	126
Various Prayers	126

Foreword

Wayne E. Oates, an academic pioneer in the fields of psychology of religion and pastoral care, saw himself first and foremost as a Christian pastor (*The Christian Pastor* was the title of his first book). Preaching scholar William Powell Tuck, Oates's pastor for more than a decade, focuses on this core dimension in his latest book, *A Pastoral Prophet: Sermons and Prayers of Wayne E. Oates*.

This engaging volume contains several of Oates's sermons and prayers. Tuck skillfully and accurately describes Oates's approach to and beliefs about preaching as addressing the deepest needs of our personal and congregational lives. Then he summarizes his assumptions about the task of preaching. While this book does pay tribute to Oates, it primarily focuses on much-needed wisdom for contemporary clerics.

The selection of sermons speaks to current issues facing today's serious seeker of mature faith for authentic living. Topics range from rootlessness of displaced persons, pursuing authenticity in identity, facing temptations, struggling with lust, and addressing a multitude of existential concerns. He speaks to matters of conflict, despair, and meaninglessness. These powerful messages grow from serious biblical deliberation, reflect sound theological reflection, and make creative use of great literature.

Tender, precious, intimate words flow from Oates's pastoral prayers that conclude this manuscript. Tuck's discussion of the role of prayer in a clergyperson's personal life and professional ministry make this section worth the read. These prayers address life in the raw moments of depression, divorce, death, and suicide. The prayers for ordinary circumstances point to Oates's wisdom about matters of the heart in the living of each day.

Parish ministers, spiritual directors, chaplains, pastoral counselors, and pilgrims on the spiritual journey will find inspiration and thought-provoking twists in this book. I will put it on the required reading list for my seminary students. I recommend it with passion.

G. Wade Rowatt
Senior Professor of Pastoral Care and Counseling
Baptist Seminary of Kentucky
ACPE Supervisor

Preface

Wayne Edward Oates (1917–1999) is considered one of the pioneers in the pastoral care and pastoral clinical movement in the United States. For thirty-eight years, as professor at the Southern Baptist Theological Seminary in Louisville, Kentucky, among his many courses he taught classes in psychology of religion, various aspects of pastoral care, the dimensions of personality, the work of the pastor, counseling in grief, marriage, etc., and clinical pastoral education. From 1974–1992 he taught at the University of Louisville Medical School as professor of psychiatry and behavioral sciences. Among his fifty-seven books are *The Christian Pastor* (which went through three revisions), *Psychology of Religion, Religious Factors in Mental Health, The Religious Care of the Psychiatric Patient, Pastoral Counseling, Behind the Masks,* and *The Confessions of a Workaholic.* He also edited many books including the Westminster's Christian Care Books and the Potentials: Guides for Productive Living. While teaching and writing, Oates also counseled privately with hundreds of persons from his home. While I was pastor at St. Matthews Baptist Church, he served as "pastoral care consultant" on the ministerial staff.[1]

Wayne Oates's legacy will continue to live on for generations through the impact he made in his classroom teaching, fifty-seven books, counseling, and lectures on the life and ministry of the pastor, the counselor, and the chaplain that were given around the world, and through his many graduate students who are ministering in various ways today. The counseling center he helped found at St. Matthews Baptist Church and the Wayne E. Oates Institute in Louisville, which continues to provide counseling guidance, seminars, and continuing education to those who draw upon its resources, will continue his influence. Among his many books on pastoral ministry, he published only one book of sermons, *The Revelation of God in*

Human Suffering. His most thorough treatment of the preaching ministry was set forth in a chapter titled "Preaching and Pastoral Care" in *Handbook of Contemporary Preaching*.[2] There he affirms the importance of preaching along with pastoral care. "Preaching and pastoral care are woven together as one spiritual tapestry," he asserts. "Therefore any discussion of preaching and pastoral care must be from a synoptic angle of vision."[3]

As a seminary professor and a professor at the University of Louisville's School of Medicine, he was asked to preach often in churches of many denominations. Although he published only a few of his sermons, several hundred copies of his sermons on a variety of subjects and Scriptures are in the Wayne E. Oates Papers in the Archives at Wake Forest University, which houses his collection. I had opportunity to look through these files and select some sermons that had not been published. Many of these sermons were typed by him or written in his own handwriting and likely were never intended to be published. Some of the sermons in the files are in outline form only. Several of the sermons in this collection that I have edited were preached at St. Matthews Baptist Church in Louisville, Kentucky, while I was pastor there; several were preached in the chapel at the Southern Baptist Theological Seminary in Louisville, and others were selected from sermons he had published earlier.

I had the privilege of serving as Wayne Oates's pastor for ten years while I was senior minister at St. Matthews Baptist Church. Although I was his pastor, he was my pastor in many ways. I continue to appreciate his support and encouragement during the many difficult years at St. Matthews Baptist Church when we were in the process of rebuilding following a devastating fire that destroyed the sanctuary, offices, and part of the educational building. This was a time of grief, anger, frustration, struggle, and challenge for me and the whole congregation. His quiet, confident support and encouragement enabled the church and me as its pastor to weather some difficult years. On numerous occasions, I invited Dr. Oates to preach or to lead us in special congregational studies. He always had a positive, uplifting, informative word of hope and guidance. This book is a small token of my appreciation for the life and ministry of Wayne Oates, which I told Pauline, his wife, I wanted to do one day in gratitude for his impact on my life and the lives of countless thousands of others. I hope other readers of these sermons and prayers will be as inspired by them as I have been.

I want to express to my friend and fellow minister, Rand Forder, who studied under Oates, my appreciation for proofreading my manuscript. I also appreciate Wake Forest University for granting me the opportunity to examine his papers in their archives. My editing of Oates's sermons and prayers was limited mostly to removing introductory or other materials that seemed to distract from the sermon itself. All royalties from this book will go to the Wayne E. Oates Institute in Louisville, Kentucky.

NOTES

1. For more details about Oates's life and ministry, see the chapter, "Wayne Oates: Pastoral Theologian," in my book William Powell Tuck, *Modern Shapers of Baptist Thought in America* (Richmond VA: Center for Baptist Heritage & Studies, 2012) 155–78.

2. Wayne E. Oates, "Preaching and Pastoral Care," in Michael Duduit, ed., *Handbook of Contemporary Preaching* (Nashville: Broadman Press, 1992) 445–554.

3. Ibid., 445.

Introduction: Wayne E. Oates as a Preacher

For a man who would become a national pastoral psychologist and religious educator, Wayne Oates had a modest beginning. He was born on June 24, 1917, in Greenville, South Carolina, to parents who had lived and worked on the edge of poverty as sharecroppers in rural Pickens County, South Carolina, and later moved to Greenville to work in the cotton mills. He was the fourth and last child in his family because his father abandoned the family for another woman when Oates was in his infancy. He was raised by his mother, his grandmother, and a sister. His mother had to work in the cotton mills to support the family. The scarcity of food, clothing, and shelter was an issue from his earliest memories, and he felt they were in bondage to poverty. He recalled that his family moved twenty-seven times before he finished high school. His widowed grandmother, who had never been to school, lived with them. She taught herself to read, spell, and write and used the same method to teach her grandson. Oates said she taught him the same way before he went to school and impressed upon him very early to love words. His teacher recognized his intellectual gifts, and he was selected in the eighth grade to serve as a Senate page for a year.

Later he would graduate from Mars Hill Junior College, Wake Forest College (now University), and Southern Baptist Theological Seminary where he would earn his BD, ThM, and ThD degrees. While a student at Wake Forest College, he married Pauline Rhodes, who was a member of his student church in North Carolina, and later they had two sons. After completing his graduate work, Oates taught at Southern Seminary from 1945–1974 and later from 1983–1992 and at the Louisville University's medical school from 1974–1992. During these years, he authored more than fifty books, counseled many persons, and lectured and preached worldwide. Oates died on October 21, 1999, at the age of eighty-one.

Wayne Oates was not known for his preaching, but mostly for his work in pastoral counseling and the number of articles and books he wrote on that topic. His experience as a pastor was limited to the pastorates of Peachtree-Bunn in Nash County, North Carolina, from 1940–1943 when he was a student and part-time professor at Wake Forest and his seminary pastorate at Union City, Kentucky, from 1943–1945. But his knowledge of pastoral ministry, including preaching, was widely acclaimed. He not only was a gifted lecturer but also was recognized as an effective preacher and often asked to preach in churches of many denominations. Some of his sermons were collected in volumes like *The Minister's Manual and Best Sermons* by James W. Cox[1] and in two books by Charles F. Kemp.[2] He also had a collection of his sermons in a book titled *The Revelation of God in Human Suffering*.[3] The sermons in this collection, Oates exclaims, are on the theme of "the stresses of life" and aim to give a common core of meaning and continuity to the sermons that were a part of his preaching ministry since his ordination as a preacher of the gospel.[4] His preaching style was a soft, conversational tone that invited the listener to join him in a quest for a "word" from God. He rarely raised his voice and never tried to use emotion to entice the listener. His outline was simple and easy to follow and his sermons always had a strong biblical focus. Most of his sermons addressed a life need of the congregation with illustrations drawn from his own experience or wide reading. He was a master storyteller and kept the attention of the listeners as they followed his real-life experience that always spoke to some listener's need that very Sunday. He believed that the sermon was "a living testimony of psychological wisdom and not a reflective essay about psychology."[5]

He felt that preaching and pastoral counseling were inseparable functions of the pastor's ministry.[6] He followed the model of Harry Emerson Fosdick and Leslie Weatherhead in preaching "life situation" sermons that always sought to relate preaching to the genuine needs of his listeners. He believed strongly that preaching could be a form of pastoral care and that many of the needs of a congregation could be addressed through the preaching of the pastor. He saw the preacher as one who appeals to the common and universal elements in the human situation, while the pastoral counselor is trying to discover the unique individuality of one person at a time and what the universals mean to him or her.[7] The sermon could also be a stimulus to encourage listeners to seek counseling from the pastor when they hear the pastor speak about loneliness, guilt, forgiveness, fear, grief, or some other need in their lives. Oates encourages the pastor not to forget that preaching and pastoral care are "relational" events: "They are face-to-face relationships between the pastor and the congregation, family, small groups, or individual."[8] The relationship needs to be one of trust and openness between the preacher and the congregation. Acknowledging his or her own humanity, the preacher joins the congregation in seeking a word from God that is directed to the preacher as well as to the congregation as he or she joins with them as a fellow pilgrim in faith.

Oates warns against what he calls "homiletical narcissism," which he sees as the preacher being authoritarian rather than authentic, focusing the content of the sermon on himself or herself, lacking empathy or sympathetic imagination where the preacher ridicules or portrays the worst-case scenario of people or where the preacher uses the sermon to vent his or her anger, disgust, and contempt. Authentic preaching in contrast with narcissistic preaching, he believes, is permeated with the simplicity and directness of Jesus and Paul. The preacher does not take himself or herself too seriously but is self-emptying rather than being self-centered. He or she has the capacity to express gratitude to and for the congregation as well as the ability to share appropriate admonition. The preacher has to acknowledge genuine humility in the quest for religious knowledge and honestly admit that he or she only knows in part. The authentic preacher is not afraid to acknowledge that he or she has not "arrived" in personal spiritual growth, but is a pilgrim like all Christians striving toward the spiritual heights.[9] In another lecture, Oates reflects on various ways a preacher might approach the "preaching event." Some approach their preaching responsibility with the central focus on the sermon itself as a craft or art without any regard where the congregation might be in their spiritual quest. Others might be concerned primarily with the response of the audience, which the preacher might manipulate to achieve a selfish end or personal gratification. Similar to the "narcissistic" preacher, some might make the preaching event a focus on the preacher himself or herself. This does not mean that there can never be a proper involvement of one's self in the sermon, but the preacher must always, according to Oates, make "the centrality of the person of Christ" outshine any personal light.[10]

Oates was keenly aware that every preacher faces the homiletical challenges to address the deepest needs of one's congregation, to probe the Scriptures correctly for a "word from the Lord," to "package" the sermon so the congregation will want to listen to it, and authentically to join her or his fellow Christians in the pilgrimage of faith. He encouraged the preacher to pray the Socratic prayer: "O Lord, give me beauty in the inner person, and may the outward person and the inward person be the same." In most of these sermons, Oates does not use inclusive language. He reflects the time in which he lived. While I have retained his language, I know that today he would be inclusive in his use of references to men and women and to God.

Notes

1. Several sermons by Oates are included in *The Ministers Manual*, 1986 ed., ed. James W. Cox (San Francisco: Harper & Row Publishers, 1986) 82–89. Illustrations and digested sermon ideas by Oates are included in other volumes of *The Ministers Manual*. Oates's sermon, "The Revelation of God in Human Suffering," is part of *The Twentieth Century Pulpit*, ed. James W. Cox (Nashville: Abingdon Press, 1978) 153–60.

2. Wayne E. Oates, "The Need for Roots," in *Pastoral Preaching*, ed. Charles F. Kemp (St. Louis MO: The Bethany Press, 1963) 126–32, and Wayne E. Oates, "The Struggle for Maturity," in *The Preaching Pastor*, ed. Charles F. Kemp (St. Louis MO: The Bethany Press, 1966) 196–208.

3. Wayne E. Oates, *The Revelation of God in Human Suffering* (Philadelphia: The Westminster Press, 1959).

4. Ibid., 9.

5. Ibid., 10.

6. Some of this material is drawn from my chapter, "Wayne Oates: Pastoral Theologian," in *Modern Shapers of Baptist Thought in America* (Richmond VA: Center for Baptist Heritage & Studies, 2012) 174–75.

7. Oates, *The Revelation of God in Human Suffering*, 11.

8. Wayne E. Oates, "Preaching and Pastoral Care," in *Handbook of Contemporary Preaching*, ed. Michael Duduit (Nashville: Broadman Press, 1992) 445ff.

9. Wayne E. Oates, "Authentic Preaching vs. Homiletical Narcissism," unpublished lecture.

10. Wayne E. Oates, "Different Approaches to the Preaching Event," unpublished lecture.

Part I: Sermons

THE NEED FOR ROOTS[1]

Preached in New York City and Washington, DC, late 1950s–early 1960s; precise date unknown

The Jews had been taken as captives of war. They were carried into Babylon, torn from the roots of their existence in their native land. The ground of their identity had been torn from beneath them. Now they were in strange territory. One of their poets wrote,

> By the waters of Babylon, there we sat down and wept when we remembered Zion.
> On the willows there
> we hung up our lyres.
> For there our captors required of us songs,
> and our tormentors, mirth, saying, "Sing us one of the songs of Zion!"
> How shall we sing the LORD's song in a foreign land? (Ps 137:1-4)

In these last words—"How shall we sing the LORD's song in a foreign land?"—the Hebrew poet stated the dilemma of all religious people of all times who have been uprooted from their native soil. To what extent did their religion depend on the soil in which it was rooted? What happens to a person's religious faith when he is no longer in his native country?

This is an imperative dilemma for you and me, for our families, and for our churches today. One out of four families will change its address this coming year, and change its address from one state of the union to another or to a foreign country. The exceptional mobility of life today, also, is not merely geographical. Persons who live in the same city all their lives will tend to change their social group. They move up or down the social ladder in such a way that the religious group of their youth will not be the spiritual community of their adulthood. A process of uprooting, transplanting, and all the hazards that go with it takes place. By social change, they will often be uprooted through education and occupation from the religion of their parents. They are faced with social uprooting in the same way that others are confronted with geographical uprooting. In many instances, both kinds of both social and geographical moving take place in the lives of the same people.

Uprooting and transplanting is a part of life. It must be faced. Abraham went out by faith from Ur of the Chaldees. The very nature of marriage causes man and woman, if they live according to God's purpose in creation, to leave father and mother and cleave to one another. As they grow older and their own children mature, they in turn have their nest torn up by the education, vocation, and marriage of their children. Furthermore, the stern injunction of the Lord Jesus Christ is that the easy securities of houses, lands, husbands, wives, children, mothers, and fathers are to be left for the greater security of rootage in the kingdom of God. Then and only then does life come into true fruitage.

In the face of the dilemmas of uprooting, people are called upon to "sing the song of their God" in strange lands. The dangers and possibilities of this uprooting in the spiritual life were the burden of concern of the poet who wrote the first psalm. Charles A. Briggs rightly translates Psalm 1:6, "He is like a tree that is transplanted by streams of water, that yields its fruit in its season, and its leaf does not wither. In all that he does he prospers."[2] Yet before the psalmist comes to this mood of affirmation, he recognizes that not all men are so. Some remain un-rooted. They wither, dry, remain fruitless, and are like the chaff that the wind blows away.

The fact remains that much of our religion depends on having an environment conducive to its growth and nurture. The burden of our text is, "Does our faith in God depend entirely upon that conducive environment of our hometown? Are the sons of Zion applicable only in the friendly territory of Zion itself? Can we stand the shock of uprooting?" The validity of our faith is tested in this shock. Plato tells the story of the Shepherd of Gyges, a young shepherd who found a ring that would make him invisible to his neighbors. This gave him the right to do as he pleased without being observed or detected. Prior to his having received this ring, he was a righteous, godly, and virtuous man. After he was freed of the scrutinizing eyes and detecting influence of his neighbors, he became an unscrupulous, ungodly, and rapacious man. This is what Albert Camus described as "achieving more than the vulgar ambitious man and rising to that supreme summit where virtue is its own reward." The reward for such virtue is the adulation of one's associates. We are told that religion at its best is what a man does in his solitude, how he handles his aloneness before God. Herein is a major test of his faith. When one is uprooted from his provincial surroundings, he no longer has to report in to mother and father, husband and/or wife, neighbor and friend; he confronts himself afresh as he really is. The conventional, routine, and habitual sources of his faith are torn away. He becomes what he really is, not what he seems to be or would like to appear to be. Otherwise courteous, unselfish, and gentle people often become rude, grasping, and harsh people when the secondary gains of approval of a known fellowship of their own personal Zion is no longer about to reward them for goodness.

On the other hand, uprooting may simply overtake some, not with actual wrongdoing but with homesickness, bereavement, and self-pity. Uprooting is particularly hard on little children and young people who are developing their sense of identity in relation to their chums and fellow schoolmates. One friend of mine in Washington—which is a city of displaced persons—moved from one side of the city to the other. It disrupted his seven-year-old son's play and school groups. He was very sad. He asked his father if they might not have a prayer room in their new home, because, he said, "We need a prayer room for times like these."

Many of us, though, as adults, do not work through our grief in fear and trembling and prayer. We simply deify the religion of our home province. We assume that there are no other places like the old places; no ways to worship other than the way they worship "back home"; no songs but the songs of Zion with which to sing glad praise to God. We react as Naaman did when the prophet Elisha healed him. He thought that only the two mules' burdens of earth upon which he had originally encountered God, his first healing experience of grace, could provide adequate nourishment for his spiritual life. He asked to take this dirt back to Syria with him. Like him, we would haul our geography around with us in our minds' eyes and never test the new soil upon which we are standing; never assess the streams of water around us for their sustaining powers for spiritual growth. We may be so impressed with the Mississippi River, the Wabash River, the Suwannee River, the Missouri River, or the Jordan River, that the Hudson River and the East River and the Harlem River or the Ohio River only cause us to weep for home.

Gross rebellion and idolatrous grief, then, are two of the negative possibilities of uprooting. But the psalmist speaks of re-rooting, transplanting, as the better way. The psalmist meditated upon the law of the Lord both day and night. He discovered in the new land of Babylon streams of living water. He re-rooted himself in the spiritual subsoil of his new environment.

When we follow his example, we can stand the shock of transplantation. We can make a living contribution to the community of which we are newly becoming a part. At the same time, we begin to discover new things about ourselves and about the nature of God himself.

The most important thing I suppose we learn about ourselves is that we are more akin to all mankind than we are estranged from and different from all mankind. As Harry Stack Sullivan says, we are more distinctly human than otherwise. The West Coast person who grew up in a community where Orientals were a threat discovers, for example, a kinship with them in New York that he did not know before. As one little Japanese boy playing with a child from a white family said, "I can't play war with my friend. He and I know each other too well. We have to go out and find some people we don't know so well to play war with and to play like we are shooting them." A Southerner from Alabama who has accustomed herself to thinking of Negroes as uneducated and uncommunicative is jarred in her presuppositions about the Negro race as a whole based upon her limited experience. Or a New Yorker visiting in Mississippi will discover that not all Mississippians are members of a hate-venting mob. The Britisher who comes to America thinking of all Americans as affluent worshipers of the almighty dollar is shaken to discover an American social worker who eats a slim helping at the local Chock Full o'Nuts and shares her funds liberally in order that her young charges might have the privilege of a religious ministry they otherwise would not get. Even in hurdy-gurdy, glittering New York, impersonal as the subway population would markedly have you believe it is, there quietly emerges a kinship system, a fellowship that is unorganized but effective, quiet but deeply penetrating. It nourishes the roots of the life of the person who will let his roots stay in one place long enough to be fed aright.

If we learn this about ourselves, then, during times of uprooting, the most important thing we learn about God is that God is not restricted to our home place. He is not too high and lifted up to become a Nazarene, but at the same time, he is Spirit. Those who worship him must worship him not on one mountain or another mountain, neither on Gerizim nor in Jerusalem, but in Spirit and in truth. He is the God "who stretches out the heavens like a curtain, and spreads them like a tent to dwell in."

He cannot be contained in any load of earth that two mules can pull. God is not another Britisher, nine feet tall. God is not a Southern plantation owner. God is in New York, but New Jersey is not west nor Boston east to him. This is the great discovery the Jews made in the exile: that God was not just in Zion and that one did not have to be in Zion to sing songs of praise and worship to him. This was the discovery about God they brought back from the exile!

These are the two things I hope we will discover as we worship quietly in our places. Right around us here in this city, in this church, we can find both soil and springs of spiritual reality whereby we may take root and grow in this community of faith. We may be alone and isolated, separated from our enduring community of faith, but here on the very ground upon which we stand God is ready and willing to reveal to us people of good will, lasting devotion, and spiritual integrity to whom we can be related. We need not forever be spiritual tumbleweeds, cast about by every wind that blows. We need not be spiritually unproductive, though we are here for only a little while. The simple fact remains that none of us has a lasting dwelling place in time. The nature of life itself is to uproot and transplant itself in order to be productive and reproductive. This is the missionary impulse and nerve of the life of the Christian community. We need not always be a guest in this church. This can be a place where we can sing a new song to the Lord. We can find sustenance, renewal, and spiritual rootage in faith here in worship.

We are a flying people who take the wings of the morning and literally fly to the uttermost parts of the sea. Yet we cannot fly away from God ever. We always fly to God. Even in our most extended journey, God is our dwelling place from everlasting to everlasting. If we make our bed in hell, he is there. Both darkness and light are alike to him. He is the ground of our being and the source of our kinship systems. We need not be lost sheep of the house of Israel because we are uprooted. We need not wither and become chaff for the wind to blow away in our self-pity, nostalgia, and separation from the accustomed environment of our home province. We need not be orphans, for God, upon the request of Jesus Christ, wills to give us the Holy Spirit. Thus we can be uprooted and transplanted. We can bring forth fruit in due season without a leaf withering.

We thank thee for the godly fellowship of the Christian faith upon which the sun never sets nor fails to rise each morning. We thank thee for thy eternal presence, that thou art always nigh. Root us and ground us in love that we may bring forth fruit in thy name. Amen.

Notes

1. Wayne Oates, "The Need for Roots," published in *Pastoral Preaching*, ed. Charles F. Kemp (St. Louis MO: The Bethany Press, 1963) 126–32.

2. Charles Augustus Briggs, *A Critical and Exegetical Commentary on the Book of Psalms*, vol.1 (Edinburgh: T. & T. Clark, 1916) 6.

2

WHAT CHRIST MEANS TO ME

"Who do you say the Son of Man is?" (Matthew 16:13)
Preached in the Chapel at the Southern Baptist Theological Seminary, Louisville, Kentucky, April, 21, 1974

I have thought about this occasion since I was asked to speak in chapel knowing that some of you are beginning your seminary work and others are preparing for graduation. For me it is also a time of a new beginning. And I said, "Well, what shall I say?" And I have one thing I want to talk about. I want to be very clear, not "perfectly" clear but just "very" clear. I want you to know very clearly what Christ means to me. And I could keep you here all day telling you what a wonderful thing he has done in my life and what he means to me, but I have picked out three of the most important things that he means to me.

The first one is that Christ is my teacher, who is always saving me through his teaching from any idol that I am tempted to worship. When I was a college student at Mars Hill in my freshman year, I read the New Testament for the first time. And I came to Mars Hill with a great central hurting in my life and that is that I was a fatherless person. And that since birth: as fathers go, I had been alone in the world. And what a great liberation from the idolatry of that sense of loss came to me when I read the New Testament and read the words of our Lord Jesus Christ and he said, "Pray to your Father who is in heaven." And I discovered who my father is. It is the God and Father of our Lord Jesus Christ. That is who my father is. And others may be reflections of him, but he is my father.

And I read in that passage also that "any man that comes after me and forsakes father, mother, brother, sister, houses, lands, children, et cetera, will find in this time a hundredfold fathers and mothers and brothers and sisters; and in the life to come—eternal life." And that's what Southern

Baptists have meant to me. That is what you mean to me—a hundredfold fathers, mothers, brothers, sisters, daughters, and sons! You are my family, the larger family of mankind. But when I find this reading, I am always aware of the demonic possessiveness of proximate concern in the face of the ultimate worship of the Lord Jesus Christ. And those of you who know me best know what a terrible suffering it was to see a son go to war, return in 1969, and what a temptation it was to worship him because I loved him so. But then came the teaching of our Lord Jesus Christ again and said he will never be free; he will never be a man if you worship him. Love him—but don't worship him. Jesus calls us from each idol that would call us and keep us, and says Christian, love me more. And now he has given my son back to me as my teacher, and I learn so much from him. And the Lord Jesus Christ teaches me through him. And he is my good friend. He is a man and not a boy.

The second thing that the Lord Jesus Christ means to me is that Christ is my healer who heals my hurts, but not just to make me feel good; he heals me in order to enable me to make the forces of disease subject to me in his name, and to enable people to grow into the fullness and the image of God in him. And from the time I was a rural pastor in eastern North Carolina with my collaboration with the medical profession, I have been astounded. I have sat in awe. I have been overwhelmed to see that by the power of the disciplined communication of the good news of God's love to sick people, they can get well. And I have felt the feelings of the disciples when I have run to him in prayer and said, "Master, the demons are subject to me." And yet I cannot rejoice because I have seen others like the epileptic boy that the disciples worked with, and I have asked him, "Master, why could they not cast it out?" And with prayer and discipline and research and a little more fasting than I have done—because gluttony, you know, is the one required sin of Southern Baptists; we have to eat, and eat, and eat to please the people—I will find out "why." And in success and failure these hands I commend to you are dedicated to bringing good tidings to the afflicted, to binding up the brokenhearted, to setting at liberty the captive, to opening prison for those who are bound, for proclaiming the year of the Lord and Savior, and for giving to those who mourn a garland instead of ashes and the oil of gladness instead of mourning, and the mantle of praise instead of a faint spirit in order that they may be called oaks of righteousness, the planting of the Lord that he may be glorified. And that's a covenant with you.

The third thing that the Lord Jesus Christ means to me is that he is my pioneer. When we look at others, we like to call them pioneers. But a pioneer who doesn't have a pioneer is in trouble. And here we sit, surrounded by a great cloud of witnesses. And the command is that we lay aside every weight and the sin which clings so closely to you and to me, and let us run with perseverance the race that is set before us, looking to Jesus the pioneer and protector of our faith, who for the joy that was set before him endured the cross, despised the shame, and is seated at the right hand of the throne of God.

Gilbert Murray has said that faith concerns the uncharted regions of life and that this is the dynamic of religion. It is to be on the periphery and on the boundary, exploring that which is not known. And the missionary frontier of today is no longer a geographical frontier. It is the frontiers of the interfaces between the professions. It is the frontiers of the interfaces between the political structures of our existence and the human needs of individuals and small groups. It is at the interfaces of the psychological differences between people of good will that make them seem to be strangers and alien to each other. These are the lines of foreign territory today. These are the lines that call for pioneering. And in the arena of pastoral research and teaching, the glorious mysteries of the ethical dimensions of man bonded to disease and social tyranny disturb me. They make me restless. And no institution can really contain that restlessness. So let's don't knock this one. But it is a restlessness that I cannot deny. And I consider this restlessness to be a sort of wild call of the sea of "unknowingness" and suffering people. And I'm with John Masefield when he says,

> I must go down to the seas again,
> To the lonely sea and the sky.
> I must go down to the seas again,
> For the call of the running tide
> Is a wild call and a clear call
> That cannot be denied.[1]

In the days of Homer the sunset was not something to be admired and made the subject of a sweet sentimental poem, or as my colleague from Brooklyn would call it, "pome." No, the sunset made even old seamen wonder what was beyond. And before the intrepid explorers of the late 1400s discovered the new world, on the coin of the Mediterranean the words *ne plus ultra* were written underneath the Pillars of Hercules. But after the discovery of the new world, they simply took the *ne* off. Because before that it was translated, "There is nothing beyond." And after that *plus ultra* meant "There is more beyond." And that "more beyondness" made people before those discoveries restless. They restlessly wondered what was beyond the sunset. And none of the comforts of their past achievements, none of the neat data that they had arrived at, none of the present prestige would satisfy that restlessness as to what lay beyond the sunset. Tennyson describes this in his *Ulysses*. Ulysses was a man of many voyages and he was talking to his men.

Tennyson catches my own spirit as I begin a new chapter in my life. And I hope he catches your spirit as you begin a new chapter in your life. You are my fellow mariners, and as Ulysses said to his people, I'll say to you:

> My Mariners, souls that have toiled and wrought and
> thought with me—
> That ever with a frolic welcome took
> The thunder and the sunshine and opposed
> Free hearts, free foreheads—you and I are old;
> Old age has yet his honor and his toil;
> Death closes all: but something ere the end,
> Some work of noble note, may yet be done,
> Not unbecoming men that strove with gods.

And then he took them down to the edge of the sea and he said to them:

> The lights begin to twinkle from the rocks:
> The long day wanes. The slow moon climbs: The deep
> Moans round with many voices. Come, my friends,
> 'Tis not too late to seek a newer world.
> Push off, and sitting well in order smite
> The sounding furrows; for my purpose holds
> To sail beyond the sunset, and the baths
> Of all the western stars, until I die.[2]

But Ulysses did not have Christ. You and I have him as the pioneer of our faith. We have him as the one who heals our diseases and teaches us in order to free us from idols. And thanks be to God for his unspeakable gift in Jesus Christ, our teacher and our healer and our pioneer. And let us work the works of him that sent us while it is yet day.

There is a hymn that expresses this truth.

Eternal Father, strong to save,
Whose arm does bind the restless wave,
Who bids the mighty ocean deep
Its own appointed limits keep;
O hear us when we cry to Thee
For those in peril on the sea.

O Trinity of love and pow'r,
Our children shield in danger's hour;
From rock and tempest, fire, and foe,
Protect them wheresoe'er they go;
Thus, evermore shall rise to Thee
Glad hymns of praise from land and sea.[3]

Notes

1. John Masefield, "Sea Fever," *The Oxford Dictionary of Quotations* (London: Oxford University Press, 1955) 334.

2. Alfred, Lord Tennyson, "Ulysses," *Anthology of the World's Best Poems*, vol. 4, ed. Edwin Markham (New York: Wm. H. Wise & Co., 1950) 1825–26.

3. "Eternal Father, Strong to Save," *The Baptist Hymnal* (Nashville: Convention Press, 1991) 69.

"The Face of Jesus Christ"[1]

2 Corinthians 4:6

Paul says, "It is God who said: 'Let light shine out of darkness; who has shone in our hearts to give the light of knowledge of God in the face of Jesus Christ." We do not often meditate upon the vision of the face of Jesus Christ. Let us do so today.

We do not have any pictures, drawings, or word descriptions of the physical appearance and the face of Jesus Christ. Yet imaginations of artists have struggled to portray his face for centuries. This is the face of a human person, Jesus of Nazareth, the carpenter's son. This is the face that on the mountain apart with Peter, James, and John was transfigured and shone like the sun. This is the face that the Apostle Paul tells us that as we ourselves with unveiled faces behold his glory, we are being changed into his likeness from one degree of glory to another (2 Cor 3:18). This is the face on which Jesus fell as he went a stone's throw from his disciples and prayed, "My Father, if it be possible, let this cup pass from me, nevertheless, not as I will, but as thou wilt." This is the face that Jesus' inquisitors covered, spat into, struck, and slapped, saying, "Prophesy to us, you Christ! Who is it that struck you?" (Matt 26:67; Mark 14:65).

This being the face of Jesus Christ and all this—and more—having happened to him, what can we say of the power of his countenance in the day-to-dayness of our sometimes humdrum existence?

The face of Jesus Christ is a real face and not a mask. Our word "personality" comes from the Latin word *persona*, meaning mask, especially as worn by actors in Greek and Roman drama. Jesus' face was not the mask of an actor. It was not the semblance or appearance of a face. It was a face made of human flesh that bled when thorns were pushed into his forehead. The Gnostics of his day and ours would have us believe that he simply seemed to be human, that he did not learn obedience through the things he suffered. He was not believed to have had a real incarnation. He only seemed to be born of a virgin mother and acted as if he were in the flesh, partaking of material nature. But the Fourth Gospel says, "The Word was made flesh and dwelt among us, full of grace and truth" (John 1:14). The First Letter of John says, "By this you know the Spirit of God: Every spirit which confesses that Jesus Christ has come in the flesh is of God . . ." (1 John 4:2).

If you and I walk in the Way of Jesus Christ, we are not putting on an act, playing a "part" called "Christian." We do not do the work of Jesus Christ as a performance. We do not, as Jesus said of hypocrites, fast, look dismal, and disfigure our faces so our fasting may be seen by other people (Matt 6:16). Rather, as our text teaches, "We have renounced the disgraceful, underhanded ways; we refuse to practice cunning or to tamper with God's Word, but by open statement of the truth, we . . . commend ourselves to every person's conscience in the sight of God." The face of Jesus Christ was "for real," and that openness demands that we reject all phoniness, playacting, grandstanding, and striking of poses of pretense. May it be said of you and may it be said of me: "That person is what he or she appears to be, a follower of Jesus Christ!" What you see is what you get. He or she is "for real."

The face of Jesus Christ is a compassionate face. Jesus focuses the gaze of his compassion upon you and me as individuals. In Mark 10:21, Jesus had just recited almost all of the commandments to the rich young man. The young man seemingly impatiently interrupted him and said, "Teacher, all these I have observed from my youth." Jesus had the option of doing what later some had been doing to Timothy when Paul told him to let no one look down upon him because of his youth. Jesus could have looked down upon this young man. He did not. He looked upon him and loved him with an *agape* love. He loved him with no self-serving needs of his own to be met. He loved him in terms of his own person as being made in the image of God. He loved him as one for whom he would later die. He loved him more than he did his own life, much more than any passing fancy or need for approval. He loved him as God loves people. Such acceptance and love is awe inspiring. For some it is terrifying and, as Emily Dickinson says, "They erect defense against love." This young man did this. He went away sorrowing, because he could not respond with a whole heart. Yet Jesus' look of compassion followed him.

The face of Jesus is a compassionate face. Many individuals come under that focused gaze of compassion. He was moved with compassion for the leper, stretched out his hand, touched the untouchable, and healed him (Mark 1:40-41). He saw a bereaved widow at Nain whose only son had died. He had compassion on her. Jesus did not look upon this widow to lust after her as a woman or to lust after her widow's money. He looked upon her with compassion as a doubly bereaved person whose husband was already dead and whose only son had just died and was being carried out. Jesus had compassion on her and brought her son back to life (Luke 7:11-15).

You and I have options as to how we look upon other people, both men and women. We can look upon them to see what they can do for us. We can look upon them as means to our goals, as tools to be used in the satisfaction of our desires. Or we can look upon them as obstacles in the way of achieving our political ambitions. Or we can simply look upon them as nonpersons, nonentities, as not even being there. Our faces reflect these motives and these valuings of persons.

But our finest option for looking upon persons is with compassion. Jesus looked upon crowds of persons and "had compassion upon them, because they were harassed and helpless, like sheep without a shepherd" (Matt 9:36). The way you look at persons, conformed to the compassionate face of Jesus Christ, transforms your relationships to them. You move from self-serving to redemptive caring; you move from littleness of self-defense to empathic participation in the otherness of people's lives. You take into yourself the treasure of the image of God in them. Your face takes on the likeness of the compassionate face of Jesus Christ.

The face of Jesus Christ is a silent face. The silence of eternity collects itself in this face of Jesus Christ. In this awesome silence, our own hearts are both comforted and confronted. The silence of Jesus' face became a deafening quietness in the last few days of his life. He had told Peter that before the cock would crow, he would deny him three times. Luke tells us that as Peter denied a third time that he knew Jesus, "while he was still speaking, the cock crowed." Then, Luke tells us, "And the Lord turned and looked at Peter" (Luke 22:61). Peter went out and wept bitterly. The silence of Jesus brought the memory of his prophecy to Peter. But did it, at that moment, bring also the promise that after Jesus' resurrection, Peter, having succumbed to temptation himself, would have both the wisdom and compassion to turn and strengthen the Son of God, "who loved me and gave himself for me" (Gal 2:20)?

The time has come, and now is the time for us to get off the fence, to quit fighting for the freedom of indecision. We look into the face of Jesus Christ and find our own real humanity mirrored in the flesh. We look into his face and find acceptance, affection, and compassion. His silent face prompts within us the growth of a wise and good conscience. His steadfast and intentional face sets the course of our lives and guides us unfailingly toward God's destiny for our whole lives and the meaning of each passing day.

Robert Browning writes in his long poem *Saul* of how David sought to heal Saul of his despairing depression with music. He played tunes that all sheep know, tunes that would make a quail leave its mate, the wise-song of the reapers, a funeral dirge, and a wedding song. Finally, a battle song was played to the sound of Saul's name. Saul stirred and his labored breathing subsided. However, nothing completely restored "Saul, the mistake, Saul, the failure, the ruin he seems now . . . to find himself clear and safe in new light and new life." David confesses his inadequacy and says,

> 'Tis the weakness in strength, that I cry for! my flesh, that I seek
> In the Godhead! I seek and I find it. O, Saul, it shall be
> A Face like my face that receives thee; a Man like unto me.
> Thou shalt love and be loved by, for ever: a Hand like this hand
> Shall throw open the gates of new life to thee. See the Christ stand![2]

Notes

1. Wayne Oates, "The Face of Jesus Christ," published in *The Ministers Manual*, 1986 ed., ed. James W. Cox (San Francisco: Harper & Row Publishers, 1986) 82–85.

2. Robert Browning, *Saul*, in *The Complete Works of Robert Browning*, vol. 4, ed. Charlotte Porter and Helen A. Clarke (New York: George D. Sproul, 1898) 85; pt. 103, lines 71–75 (http://www.bartleby.com/236/103.html).

The Providence of God and Our Temptations

Genesis 22:1-19; 1 Corinthians 10:12-13

Preached in St. Matthews Baptist Church, Louisville, Kentucky, August 5, 1990

"No temptation has overtaken you that is not common to all people. God is faithful and will not let you be tempted, tested, stressed, or burdened beyond your strength. God will, with the temptation, test, stress, or burden also provide a way of escape, or, as one translator puts it, 'Make an end to it so that you can stand up under it.'" This is one of the most cherished texts in the New Testament.

In the first place, it reminds us that regardless of the temptation, or the burden that we are having to carry, we are not alone in carrying it. All of humankind has temptation, stress, testing, and burdens. All God's children got troubles! We have our burden in common with all humankind. We can sing together with them "the still, sad music of humanity" as Wordsworth puts it. The challenge is that we join the human race, that we are no exceptions to human suffering and to human testing. We would like to think that we are an exception and we ask when burdens fall upon us, "Why has this happened to me?" A good answer is, "We are no exception." A better answer is that we are not alone, that if we look around us, there are others sharing burdens with us.

The second big message in this passage is that the text reminds us that God is faithful and knows better than we do how much temptation, testing, stress, or burden we can stand. God will not permit us to be loaded down beyond our endurance. The metaphor that is most applicable here is from the world of physics. How much will a load-bearing beam stand? If we could look up and see the beams that are in the ceiling of this building, some architect had to know how much weight would be upon them and how much of a beam it would take to hold them. God is the great architect of our lives. He knows how much we can carry.

I recall a quotation from Archibald MacLeish's play on Job. It is called *J B*—Job. One of the characters, Mr. Zuss, with indignation and rhetoric, speaks of the frailty of man's efforts in general as he reflects on J B:

> Loves a woman who must sometime, somewhere
> Later, sooner, leave him
> Fixes all his hopes on little children
> One night's fever or a running dog
> Could kill between dark and day;
> Plants his work, his enterprise, his labor,
> Here where every planted thing
> Fails in time, but still he plants it . . . .[1]

Later J B, reflecting on the suffering and losses he has endured, cries,

What I can't bear is the blindness—
Meaninglessness—the numb blow
Fallen in the stumbling night.[2]

J B's question is our question. How much can a person bear? That is the question.

We as preachers are masters at laying upon you as laypersons tremendous expectations without asking how you are going to bear them. I recall being the chaplain in Kentucky State Hospital near Danville in 1947. Preaching to an audience of 500 mental patients is an experiment, an adventure. It is a heady adventure because they are not all controlled like you are. They will interrupt you without asking to do so, ignoring all of the canons of courtesy. After you have done this for a while it becomes refreshing because many of their questions are very much to the point. I was preaching on Mother's Day. I was telling them of the scriptural passage that there comes a time when children have to pull away and leave father and mother and that the parent who has brought them to maturity has to put up with seeing them leave. As I got into this, I waxed somewhat eloquent. I got interrupted. A Southeast Kentucky woman stood up and said, "Preacher, what you are saying is very, very nice. What if it just ain't in you to do it?" Not a bad question! The fact and the truth of the matter is that in bearing some of the burdens that we have to bear, it ain't in us to do it. We don't have the strength and God speaks to us and says, "In my strength is your weakness made perfect." God provides us with the strength to bear up under that burden. That was the thought that came to me. I just stopped preaching what I had planned and entered into conversation with this very wise but very disturbed mother who knew far more about what I was talking about than I did. She was a mother and it made a difference.

The third message that this text reminds us of is that God is our provider. God in his providence will provide a way out of the temptation, the stress, the testing, and the burden. That is the core message of this passage. The element in it that rarely gets mentioned is that God is the provider for us in the face of temptation, that we are not alone, that there are fellow sufferers with us, that God knows how much we can bear, and God is providing a way through the temptations and struggles that you are carrying. More of you brought severe burdens here this morning than didn't. I encourage you to put them down a while and rest yourself here and hear the word of the Lord that in your feeling alone, the rest of us are with you. In your feeling that you have had more than you can take, God knows how much you can take and God will provide strength for the living of these days.

However, this text is ordinarily taken out of its context and that context is extremely important. The context of the whole chapter 10 is set in conditions in which Paul alerts his reader to the temptation of letting the ordinary testing of life push us into idolatry. Idolatry is putting anything or anyone less than God in God's place at the center of our lives. Paul cites three examples. The first is when the children of Israel in Moses' absence built themselves a golden calf and ate and drank and made burnt offerings to it. The second is in Numbers 25:1-18 where the Israelites turned to the idols of the Moabites and began to worship them. Twenty-five thousand of them died of the plague. The third one is in Numbers 16 in which the people of Israel were ungrateful for the manna and called it "worthless food." Many of them died because of serpents that bit them. God provided a golden serpent and said if they would look upon it, they would be healed. As you would believe it, they turned the golden serpent into an idol and worshiped it. It was really never destroyed in the minds of the Israelites until Jesus said, "As Moses lifted up the serpent in the wilderness; even so I will be lifted up and if I be lifted up all people who will come to me will be saved." Finally, the idolatry of the serpent was put to rest. In the next verse after our passage of Scripture, Paul says, "Therefore, shun the worship of idols" (1 Cor 10:14).

Nowadays we don't worship golden serpents, and we don't worship idols like the Hebrews and Greeks did—graven images. But we do worship idols. Let's take the life of an adolescent, a young person, in his or her struggle for independence from parents. He or she can become an idolater of their peer group, become a slave to what the other kids think, say, and do. They can become tempted by the misuse of automobiles, by premature sexual activity, or by alcohol and drugs. In their effort to be independent, they become idolatrously dependent. Some of them do, but not all of them—for heaven's sake, no! I am astounded at how dedicated some of the adolescents who give me the privilege of talking with them are and how much heat and gaff they put up with from their peer group. So let's don't make blanket judgments about adolescents.

Then there is the idolatry of our work. Our workplace becomes the passion that excludes all else. Today those of us who work in the Southern Baptist Convention are being sorely tempted—tested, tried, burdened by the controversy that goes on in the Southern Baptist Convention.[3] We are being asked to bow down and worship words that are not in the Bible, to say "uncle" to the power broker, and to let them be our Baal. However, there are still among us, as the Lord told Elijah, seven thousand prophets who have neither bowed the knee to Baal nor kissed him. We are being tempted to assume that the Southern Baptist Convention is a flat earth and there is nothing beyond the Southern Baptist Convention. That is idolatry of a convention. It takes God's place. But God will not let us be tempted above that which we are able. God will reveal to us that the Southern Baptist Convention is a speck in the galaxies of the universe of people on this earth and in the galaxies of the universe beyond this earth. So let's don't despair and let's don't bow down and worship. There are seven thousand Southern Baptist prophets who have not bowed their knee to Baal, not kissed him anywhere. And I don't intend to bow down and worship and say "uncle" to anybody!

Then there is retirement. When a person has made his or her work the be-all and end-all of their existence and they retire, they are likely to say, "They have taken my Lord away, and I do not know where they laid him." Work won't stand that much. There are whole new vistas of service out there for the retired person, and we have retired people in this church who are proving it. I am astounded at the recovery of energy and life I see in people whom I know who are retired.

But most of all, there is parenthood and the idolatry of children small and large—the great temptation! We have a case history of that in Abraham. Let us put ourselves in Abraham's place. He and Sarah had not been able to have children. Then comes along this wee lad, Isaac. Any of us would be tempted to make such a little lad the center of our existence. I know my great temptation has been the worship of my own sons and of my wife. I recall very well when we brought the first one home. The next morning after we brought him home, after having slept a very skimpy night, I went to the mirror to shave. It came to me that something had happened in the birth of this son that could never unhappen. As long as he lived into all eternity, I would be his father, and as long as I lived into all of eternity, he would be my son. An event that important is likely to make you fall down on your knees and worship the little baby. But when he was nineteen years old, he went to war in Viet Nam and I was devastated. I read that passage in the Scripture where Jesus said, "There is no man that hath left house, or brethren, or sisters, or father, or mother, or wife, or children, or lands, for my sake, and the gospel's, but he shall receive an hundredfold now in this time... (Mark 10:29-30 KJV)." It meant to me that I should not worship this little boy. Otherwise, I would ruin his life. That is the plight that Abraham was in. God provided a lamb in Isaac's stead. Abraham and Isaac came down from the mountain. Abraham had an enlarged and changed conception of God. God was not a God who required the sacrifice of children. Abraham had a different relationship to Isaac. He could love him, but he did not let him take God's place. So he named the place Jehovah-Jireh—God has provided. The providence of God gave us our Lord Jesus Christ. We take the lamb given to Abraham as a symbol of the provision of the Lord Jesus Christ, who is the Lamb of God that takes away the sins of the world. He is the focus of our worship, not the worship or idolatry of our children.

NOTES

1. Archibald MacLeish, *J B* (Boston: Houghton Mifflin Co, 1956) 47.

2. Ibid., 108.

3. This reference was to the controversy in the Southern Baptist Convention at that time in which denominational leaders and trustees of convention institutions were trying to force seminary professors and other convention workers to submit to a creed of biblical inerrancy and infallibility or lose their positions.

The Better Way: The Ethic of Wholeness[1]

Matthew 5:29-30; 18:8-9

These two verses of Jesus' teaching in Matthew 5:29-30 are pushed out of your and my attention by the glittering example of sexual lust that precedes them in the Sermon on the Mount. The same teaching is also found in Matthew 18:8-9 after Jesus interrupts the disciples' questions about who is greatest in the kingdom of God. The metaphor of plucking out one's eyes or cutting off one's legs or hands is rarely applied to the lust for power. Yet, in both references, they are two of the most powerful verses in Jesus' teaching, powerful because they have Jesus' way to health, holiness, and wholeness. Taken literally, and apart from the Spirit of Christ, they have a lethal message. Literalism or concreteness is a hallmark of the young child's thinking and the thinking of the mentally ill adult. When literalized, these two texts have set great tragedy into motion. I have seen acutely ill persons who interpreted this text literally for themselves. In acting upon their literal interpretation, they plucked out their eyes or they cut off their hands.

In neither instance, then, whether a little child's literalism or the concrete thinking of the psychotic person, can we find the better way of which Jesus speaks. To the contrary, he speaks of the worth of your and my living. But there's a rub here. The Matthew account prescribes a specific, face-to-face appeal to listening and teachability as a process. If a member is offending you, go to him or her alone and see if you can get them to listen. If this does not work, take another Christian with you, and see if that person will listen. Only then do you bring the matter before the congregation or a small group of the congregation. You take these steps, if you take the Bible seriously, before you consider that person as an outsider.

However, today we do not go this courageous, face-to-face way. Power-hungry people reverse the process. They go to a convention with a resolution first, then someone suggests a committee, then two people attempt to deal with the person, and the two contending persons meet face to face after all of the "little ones" have been caused to stumble. The latter is a bitter way. It does not often happen. An example of this is found in the piecemeal interpretation of the Scriptures being thrust at us today. A struggle for political power centers on the Bible. Jesus' ethic of wholeness applies here. You and I as interpreters of the word of God, both in our understanding of the Bible and in the walk of life we live out before people, are called to see life steady and whole. We are, if we have integrity, bound by ordination, biblical study, and prayer to declare the whole counsel of God. To take a piece or part of God's kerygma that fits our fancy and desire to rise up over the whole people of God is sin. Granted, we shall always know in part and prophesy in part until that which is perfect, complete, and whole is come. Yet we need not become peddlers of half-truths, which Plato said are the worst form of a lie.

This is especially true when we presume as I am now to stand before a people of God to interpret the Scriptures. If you ask me at this moment if I believe what the Bible teaches, I respond by saying that my life as a whole is contrasted with its being shaped, dominated, ruled, and ruined by a part of life, whether it is the lust for sex, power, or anything else, such as revenge. "It is better that you lose one of your members than that your whole body go into Gehenna," Jesus said. This is an ethic of wholeness, the essence of Christ's "better way," as opposed to the self-destructiveness of permitting a segment, a piece, and a part of life to destroy your and my whole life. It is rooted and grounded in the great commandment of the consecration of the whole life to God in Christ as the better way of holistic ethical living, health of being, and salvation. In this better way of Jesus Christ, you and I consecrate the whole of our being to one God, rather than this part to that god, that part to another god, and each of the other parts to as many other gods. To worship the Lord Jesus Christ with a whole heart, free of idolatry, is the way to wholeness, integration of personhood, and healthy holiness before God and our neighbor. Jesus illustrates this better way in two situations of life.

1. The covetousness of lust. The first of Jesus' two specific applications of this better way, the ethic of wholeness, is centered on the sexual lust of man for a woman and/or the struggle for power to be the greater in the kingdom of God. In the Great Commandment, he says a person is to love God with his whole heart, the seat of his emotions, wishes, and desires. He is to love his neighbor as himself. Yet the covetous lust of a man for a woman divides and adulterates his love of God. Lust treats the woman, his neighbor, as an object, a thing, a means, not as a neighbor, a person, a being made in the image of God.

When this happens, the sexual desires of a person—man or woman—take charge of the whole life. Sexual preoccupation crowds out and hinders the total life. All decisions are made with sexual intent in mind. The sexual partner, in turn, has the same thing happen to him or her as a consenting partner. However, Jesus, contrary to contemporary attempts to locate the origin of sin in women, fixes the prime responsibility in men—as revolutionary a teaching in his day as in ours. (See Rom 12:1-2; 1 Pet 1:14-16.)

In our present day, the horrible antithesis of such consecration splashes across our newspapers and television screens daily. Its gruesome results appear in our hospital emergency rooms. It has even broken out in daycare centers and kindergartens. I speak here of rape of women and the sexual abuse of children, both boys and girls. A worker in the rape relief center or in a hospital emergency room does not have trouble affirming Jesus' teaching that it is better that the person not have a sexual life than to destroy his or her own and other people's whole lives with it. The sexual exploitation of women and children is terrible when found among those who profess no religious faith. How very like the Corinthian church it is today, however, for sexual exploitation to be done in the church, by leaders of groups in the church, all in the name of sentimental, grotesque caricatures of the Christian faith.

2. *The pressure of power needs.* Jesus' second example, of the metaphor of the whole life being better without a part causing the whole to perish, centers on the competitive lust for power in the church. "Who is greatest?" In his book *The Churches the Apostles Left Behind* in which he interprets Matthew 18, Raymond Brown says,

> The answer to the question of who is the greatest in the Kingdom (or the church where the gospel of the Kingdom is proclaimed) is given through the example of the little child. This is not because, as romantics would have us think, the little child is thought of as lovable, or cuddly, or innocent, but the child is helpless and dependent, with no power.[2]

Jesus warns against scandalizing "one of these little ones" in the pell-mell dash for power in the church. It is better to have a millstone around the neck and be cast in the sea. The person who causes one of these to sin is a part of the body of Christ to be severed like a hand or foot that has risen up against the common good.

Readily you say that this is a two-edged sword. One can say that another who does not believe as he or she does should be cut off from the "land of the unfailingly true." I will tell you, if I can learn the whole truth of the whole Bible on any one subject that matters to the faith and practice of the Christian life, I will take it as the unfailing and eternal truth. However, if you ask me if I believe each part of the Scripture is infallible apart from the rest of the Bible, I will say that you have asked me to enter into a pact with the devil. For, as Shakespeare says, "The devil can cite Scripture for his purpose."[3] Such citing of Scripture usually hides two grains of wheat in two bundles of chaff, as Shakespeare again says. Such piecemeal interpretations on critical issues like divorce, the place of women, and so on are "flamingo" exegesis. The flamingo bird is fond of standing on one leg with its head under its wing to rest. The flamingo interpreter of the Scripture stands on one text and hides his or her head from the rest of the completing testimony of the Scripture as a whole.

Our prayer as seekers after the whole counsel of God is that we will not rest or make peace with this piecemeal exegesis. If we are called to be ministers, we take our visions of the call of God into the discipline of three to seven years of biblical, theological, historical, and pastoral study. We meditate on the Scriptures day and night. We refuse upon graduating to bow the knee to the golden calf of catchwords in order to capture positions of petty power on the flat earth of our little denominational scheme of things. We are committed in the name of the Lord Jesus Christ to communicate to the limits of our being the truth, the whole truth, and nothing but the truth from God's word. We refuse to cause one of the little ones of Jesus Christ to stumble. For he has told us, and it is ever before us, what is the better way. The better way is to sustain the whole life rather than be idolaters of any part of life. We are to love no other gods before him.

Notes

1. Wayne Oates, "The Better Way: The Ethic of Wholeness," published in *The Ministers Manual*, 1986 ed., ed. James W. Cox (San Francisco: Harper & Row Publishers, 1986) 87–89.

2. Raymond Brown, *The Churches the Apostles Left Behind* (Mahwah NJ: Paulist Press, 1984) 140.

3. William Shakespeare, *The Merchant of Venice*, Act l, scene 3, line 99.

The Ministry of Encouragement

Isaiah 40:27-31; Romans 15:1-6

Preached in St. Matthews Baptist Church two years after the fire destroyed their building, January 29, 1984

You and I as a congregation, since January 10 two years ago, have been on a survival school mission. We have been at the business of surviving as a church. We have been to survival school. In the United States Military, United States Navy, Air Force, Army, Marines, when people are definitely slated to go into combat, a new type of training is ordered up for them. It is called SERE (survival, evasion, resistance, and escape). It is training in survival. If one is separated from his unit, given a knife and a piece of parachute cloth, he is expected to survive in a desert area for days upon days upon days upon days with nothing to eat, living off the land on which he stands. If he is on the verge of being captured, he is trained to evade those who would capture him. If he is actually about to be captured and there is no way to evade, he is trained to resist those who would capture him. And if indeed they do capture him, he is trained to escape from those who capture him. It's survival, evasion, resistance, and escape.

You and I had our church burned down and we have been through all the stages of massive stress as a people of God. There are three major stages to stress, as Hans Selye the great physiologist from Toronto tells us. The first one is shock and alarm. And we were in shock for weeks upon weeks, hardly able to believe what had happened to us. We gave ourselves in hyperactive work to put our community back together again. The church was alive and well, though its building had burned down. We worked tirelessly. I never saw such an expenditure of energy as I saw while we were shocked and alarmed. Then we developed ways of resistance, the second stage of stress. We have been resisting dissolution as a church. We have built, for example, and are building a church, not just for replacement purposes. Anybody could do that. But with Together We Build and the tithes and offerings we are giving, we have built for the future for people who will be in this congregation long after some of us, who speak and listen now, will be dead. We came to terms with our own finitude, our own mortality. We will not be here forever, but the church's walls shall stand whether we are here or not. Now that was resistance par excellence, and you are to be congratulated on that!

But now, my friends, we are in the third stage of stress. We are exhausted. We are tired. We have seen enough to discourage us. Exhaustion has set in. Our spirits are tired. As we go from week to week and see inch to inch of the building go up, we say, "How long, O Lord? How long before we will be back into our building?" If we forget this building, Lord, your temple, let our tongues cleave to our mouth. Let's keep on praying that we will be able to do what we set ourselves to do. We stretch our budgets, we stretch our facilities, and we face the frustrations of being in borrowed quarters. We become exhausted. We become discouraged.

One advantage of this, and I like to see the advantage in the worst sorts of things, is that it has made us as a people able to see what big problems are as distinguished from little ones; what important problems are as distinguished from trivial ones. I can remember before the church burned down how we were worrying because people couldn't find a seat in a crowded building. But when a whole congregation can't find a seat, nobody worries about one person not being able to find a seat! It reminds you of Dennis the Menace when he came in out of a big rainstorm and said to his mother, "A big rainstorm sure takes the fun out of playing with a squirt gun." And a big fire sure takes the fun out of some of the petty things that we worried about before that happened.

But another learning experience is that exhaustion calls for encouragement. Encouragement means putting heart into people. It means giving them strength for the living of this day. Therefore, my purpose in this sermon is that by the power of the Lord Jesus Christ, as his messenger to you today, I may bring to you a ministry of encouragement. I want to come alongside you to brace you up. I want to let you know that both you and I have springs of encouragement that we have only begun to tap. Real heart is out there even though we are exhausted. Those springs of encouragement are ready to give you and me a steady supply of heart for completing the task that we have at hand.

Your need and my need as leaders and burden bearers in this church is for encouragement in time of exhaustion. It reminds me of a Charles Schulz cartoon. And as long as Bill Tuck can quote and footnote Charles Schulz, I thought I had the right to do so too. So I will exercise that privilege now. Snoopy is the World War I Flying Ace. I can identify with that. In the second frame of the comic he is moving among his men and he says, "The men need bracing up, the poor blighters! They have had a lot of discouragement." The next frame shows Snoopy, the World War I Flying Ace, leaning with his head against his doghouse with a tear going down his cheek and saying, "But who braces up a World War I Flying Ace?"

Well, today if you ask, "Who braces me up?" I come in the name of the Lord Jesus Christ. I come in the power of the Holy Spirit to say, "I do." That is my job today! There are four springs of encouragement to which I want to call your attention.

The first one is that we have an eternal reservoir of encouragement in the kind of God we have. When people tell me they do not believe in God I ask them, "What kind of God do you not believe in?" Because chances are I won't believe in that kind of God anyhow, either. This God we have is not just any old god. He is special. He is the one who is the God of all comfort, who in the Holy Spirit comes alongside us as the Comforter, as the Paraclete, the one who stands beside us and steadies us. We find that kind of God described in Isaiah:

> Have you not heard, have you not known that the everlasting God is the creator and the ruler of the earth? He fainteth not and neither is weary. He gives strength to those who faint. Even young people will faint and utterly fall. But they that wait upon the LORD shall have their strength renewed. They shall run and not be weary. They shall walk and not faint. They shall mount up with wings as eagles. Their youth will be renewed.

That is the kind of God we have. That is the kind of God that the Apostle Paul worshiped. After Paul had been through the wringer of the experience of trial with Ananias, he was taken back to his prison cell under heavy guard lest people kill him for having enunciated his belief in the resurrection. And that time, in his loneliness and in his deprivation and sadness, the Lord came and stood by him and said, "Take courage, you have testified about me at Jerusalem, so you must bear witness also of me at Rome" (Acts 23:11). That's the kind of God we have. He stands by us when we are totally isolated and alone under the hammer and the duress of stress. He stands by us and says, "Take courage."

This is the kind of God who is not mocked by circumstances. God is not mocked, and those of us who sow our lives related to and in devoted commitment to God will reap eternal life. But those of us who sow our lives for the temporary, short-term, fleshly desires of the moment will be destroyed. But then Paul says, "Let us not be weary in well-doing for God is not mocked. We shall reap in due season if we faint not" (Gal 6:7-9). That is the source of encouragement we have in the kind of God we have.

The second source of encouragement is that God has given us the Scriptures as an ever-ready and unlimited renewable resource of energy in steadfastness and encouragement. As we bathe our minds, tired, grimy, and dusty as they are from effort, in the Psalms, for example, they let us know that we are not alone. And if we are alone, we are alone for but a little while. As Isaiah puts it, "for a brief moment I forsook you, but with compassion I will gather you again." If you feel forsaken by God, wait a moment, and you will be gathered again.

The disciples were discouraged after the crucifixion of Jesus. They were gathered in one place to comfort and sustain each other, and the power of the Holy Spirit came upon them. Two of them, you remember, were walking upon the road to Emmaus. They had heard of great things that had happened in Jerusalem. They were talking vividly with one another about it. Suddenly they realized that they were not alone in their journey. A stranger came and walked with them. They came to the evening hour. It was time to eat. They turned aside to their dwelling. He turned aside with them. They broke bread together. In the breaking of bread, they were known of him and he of them, as he taught them the Scriptures. Then he disappeared from them. They said, "Oh, how our hearts did burn within us as he taught us and opened our eyes to the meaning of the scriptures." Their hearts were made new by the teaching of the Scripture. This is the source of renewal for St. Matthews Baptist Church when we get tired, the renewal that comes from the teaching of the Scriptures.

In a community such as this, there is a third source of encouragement. You find a source of encouragement in leaders who inspire you. They invest confidence in you and put heart into you. They are Barnabas-like people who are your leaders. They are people whom you have chosen as your leaders. They are people whom you have decided you can trust. They are people who believe in you when you don't believe in yourself. They are people who sense when you are discouraged and stand by you. They are like Barnabas. The name Barnabas means "the son of encouragement." He was the man who, when the church at Antioch needed someone to go on mission for them, went up into Tarsus and found the rejected Apostle Paul. He brought him back and stood witness for him. He recommended him to the church at Antioch; they laid their hands upon both of them under the direction of the Holy Spirit and sent them out. It was Barnabas who was Paul's son of encouragement. When they were on another journey, they took John Mark with them. Paul was not all that good at encouraging people at times, particularly John Mark. He didn't want anything to do with him. But Barnabas came into sharp contention with Paul, stood him down, and said, "I will stand by John Mark." It seemed that he had the capacity always to stand by the underdog. He had the capacity to see something good in people when others could see nothing. He saw the pure gems of possibilities. He was a son of encouragement. He elicited possibilities out of John Mark, who is the person who is reported to be the author of our oldest Gospel, the Gospel of Mark.

I can recall a Sunday school teacher in a church in Kannapolis, North Carolina, where I worked for two years as a cotton mill weaver. I went to Sunday school to this man's class. He was a Barnabas if there ever was one. His name was Zettie Walters. Out of that man's Sunday school class have come more than forty young persons who have entered full-time Christian service and who have been encouraged by that man. I was one of them. You see, we have leaders who are not slacked out when the going gets rough. They get, as [Robert] Schuller [the former senior minister of the Crystal Cathedral, Garden Grove, California] says, tough and hang in there and hang in there with you. There are leaders like that in this church. I have found them. I have turned to them. They have sustained me in difficult hours. You can find them. Many of you have found them and you thank God for them because they put heart into you.

Finally, we have another reservoir of encouragement in the powerful fellowship of believers that we are. The people in this church are no summer-time patriots. I have been in many churches but none who, not only on Sunday merely, but during the week, work harder to put heart into those who are in times of adversity. This is not just people who are sick. I bear witness to that now, but it is people with perplexities in business, family, and community. The amount of encouragement that goes on in this congregation would stagger you to know of it. Yet these people do not let one hand know what the other one is doing as they do it. Only God knows. You are a church that has taken the infection, envy, little-mindedness, and cattiness of a gossipy world and through the power of your consecration to Jesus Christ have turned it into wise concern for and ministry to people who are hurting. By the power of consecration to Christ, you have taken the same information that others would have heard as gossip and turned it into a ministry of encouragement. You reach out to people of all walks of life. St. Matthews Baptist Church is not a club. You are a fellowship of faith that now and again bursts out from your own boundaries and energizes others with the encouragement with which God has encouraged you.

This is the season, isn't it, for jumping an engine that won't run with jump cables? This is the season for it—when we are still recovering from our great tragedy. You can see it happening anywhere during winter but particularly very cold days. During the hot spell last summer, it was not the season for jump cables. I had no way of knowing that it was the season for jump cables. I came out of the cleaners in St. Matthews on a Saturday. Two burly young men approached me. They looked tough! I said, "Well, Lord, this is it! I'm gonna be mugged! Let's see what happens." I braced myself. They came to me face on and said, "Sir, could you help us? Our car won't start. Would you let us take our jump cables and jump the power from your battery to ours to start it?" I heave a sigh of relief. Most certainly, gladly! I wiped all three clammy brows! They jumped their battery.

The ministry of encouragement is like that. When we are most scared and things are going roughest and things won't move, we encourage each other by lending each other some of our energy. We put power into each other literally. May God, by reason of the God he is, by the steadfastness and encouragement of the Scriptures, by the power of leaders whom he has chosen, and by the power of his body that is the fellowship of this church, root you and ground you in encouragement. Take heart! The Apostle Paul had gone through shipwreck and his life had been hazarded, but he came up on the road, the Appian Way near the Three Taverns. In the twenty-seventh chapter and the fifteenth verse of Acts it says, "the people of the church of Rome came out to greet them and when he saw them, Paul thanked God and took heart." Every time you come to this church or see each other, I want you to thank God and take heart, because God so wills it.

The Church: A Many-splendored Fellowship

Galatians 5:16–6:6

Preached at St. Matthews Baptist Church, Louisville, Kentucky, November 10, 1985

As we, Sunday after Sunday in the past few weeks, have meditated upon the meaning of the windows in our church, I have been filled with awe—with the splendor, the radiance, and the grandeur of the message that they communicate. I wonder if you have had a similar experience to mine. Each time I fix my attention on any one of these windows, I see something new that I have not seen before. I am impressed that these windows are symbolic of the meaning of the fellowship of our church. They communicate to us a many-splendored gospel of the Creation and the Redemption and the Work of the Holy Spirit in the world. As I thought on speaking with you this morning, I said, "Why not this subject: 'The Church: A Many-splendored Fellowship'?"

The Scripture that has been read begins with the injunction that we walk in the Spirit and by the Spirit of God, that we do not gratify the desires of the flesh. It is important for us to get it clear at the outset as to what Scripture means by the flesh and the Spirit. Ordinarily we Westerners have had it woven into the fabric of our minds that Plato was right when he said that the body was one thing and the spirit is another. Therefore, we ordinarily identify the flesh with anything that refers to our bodily desires. That is the farthest from the mind of the New Testament. The flesh refers to a corruptible way of life lived in alienation from God, out of fellowship with God, and according to our own headstrong idolatries, enmities, strife, jealousies, anger, selfishness, dissension, party spirit, envy, drunkenness, and carousing and the like. It binds up all the pride and vainglory of human life into one word—flesh. To live by the Spirit is to live a life in fellowship with God. It means that the desires and wishes of our own self-centeredness have been crucified along with Christ in his crucifixion, in the faith that, having done so, God by his Spirit will raise us to walk in the newness of life and to walk in the fruits of the Spirit. These are love, joy, peace, patience, kindness, goodness, faithfulness, gentleness, and self-control, against which there is no law. When we do that together, as a people of God in the way of the mystical life of the church itself, we become a many-splendored fellowship on this earth.

Then Paul goes on to lay out clearly several facets of that splendor. In Galatians 6, it follows as day does night what the fruits of the Spirit do in our practical life.

We see, in the first place, that the church is a fellowship of fault and trespassing: "Brethren, if a person is overtaken in any trespass, you who are spiritual restore that person in a spiritual gentleness." In a crowd as large as our church, "No Trespassing" signs are always at risk. You and I as Christians can indeed put up our territory around us with signs that say "No Trespassing." But the likelihood of those signs getting ignored is high in a crowd. Trespasses do happen because we are not a perfect people. And I am glad that St. Matthews is not a perfect people because you make me feel so much at home among you. Because none of us is perfect.

I remember our being on vacation once when our sons were quite small boys. We went down to the beach in North Carolina and were talking to a man who conducts deep-sea fishing trips out on the ocean. He was a sunburned, gnarled man. As I looked at him, I noticed on his hand a large, beautiful diamond. I said, "That is a perfectly beautiful diamond that you have on your finger." He said, "I was a jeweler in Durham before I took up this job. I decided to come down here and do what I enjoyed. This is the one thing I brought with me from the jewelry store—this ring. But I want to tell you it is not perfect. You said it was perfect, but it isn't." He said, "Only rings that are made by people are perfect. Industrial diamonds are perfect. But the ones God makes are imperfect. Each has a flaw in it so God can tell us apart." That is a truth I have never forgotten. Isn't it true that our strengths, when turned at another angle, become our Achilles' heels? The very genius that makes us individuals is also a source of fault in us. Paul instructs us that if we overtake each other in a fault or a trespass or a sin, we are to restore each other in a spirit of gentleness.

In the second place, the church is a many-splendored fellowship in that it is a self-examining fellowship. Paul inspires us to look to ourselves when we find a brother or sister in fault lest we also be tempted. Here you see the metaphor not of the imperfect diamond but the one James speaks of when he says that we function a lot like looking at a mirror. We can be gentle in our restoration of each other because we look at ourselves in a mirror when we see their faults. Look to yourself! James says that it is easy for us when we look at ourselves to be like people who observe themselves in a mirror and then go away and at once forget what they are like. The faults of other people are mirrors. They reflect back to us that which we despise in ourselves. Hence we are more impatient with them and deceive ourselves because we see in them our own faults. As I like to say when I point the finger at you, there are always three more pointing back at me. So in order to be gentle with myself, I always use my left hand because there are fewer fingers of self-condemnation! The church is a fellowship of self-examination.

In the third place, the church is a fellowship of shared burdens. "Bear ye one another's burdens and so fulfill the law of Christ." In the passage in the fifth chapter, Paul talks about the law. The whole book of Galatians is concerned with the life of the Spirit verses the life of the law. Now he introduces a higher law—the law of Christ, which is the law of bearing one another's burdens and so fulfilling the law of Christ. We bear with each other's faults. We share each other's loads. That is what our stewardship commitment day is all about. Every one of us is bearing his or her share of the load of looking after each other. I am a grandfather. I don't have any little children at home who need to be taught by a church. But in the fellowship of being a Christian in a church, every little child in a church calls for my support of that little child whose parents may be struggling much, much harder to make a living than I am. I remember how someone cared for our sons when we were struggling hard to make a living. Now it is time for us to help others even as earlier we were helped.

This past October 1, Pauline and I had the marvelous experience of going back to Mars Hill College in North Carolina, which I entered in 1936, to give a Founder's Day address. Early that morning I got up and took a long walk alongside the football field. They still have some of the old wooden bleachers we had then. I remembered how, in working on the grounds crew, a group of us were assigned the job of picking those wooden bleachers up and moving them from one side of the field to another. It took about twelve of us—three on each corner. Those of us on one corner began to notice that our eyes were bulging as we lifted our end of it. Then we put it down to rest a little while. We got crafty. We began to notice what was happening. The three guys opposite us were going down about five seconds faster than we were and tilting it in our direction. They looked rather serene. They looked comfortable. But then we set the whole bleacher down and called off that particular game and said, "Everybody has got to carry his load." We bear one another's burdens. We don't pitch it on each other. That is the splendor of the fellowship of St. Matthews Church. We carry it together.

Let me speak now of a fourth dimension of this many-splendored church. It is a fellowship that transforms competition into creative work. Let each one of you test his or her own work, and then the reason to boast will be in himself or herself alone and not in a neighbor, says Paul. Competition can become so pathological in our society that we cannot function at the task that is ours due to comparing ourselves with other people. We compare ourselves with each other and lose the radiance of our life together as the people of God. But Paul is saying here that each of us in testing our own work can hold it up to God and say, "Let the beauty of the Lord be upon us and the works of our hands. Let your beauty be upon it." Because we hold it up to God alongside each other and do not compare ourselves unfavorably or other people unfavorably with us, fellowship in the Spirit of the living God in Jesus Christ takes our competitiveness and transforms it into collaboration with each other. Each glories in the work of the other rather than cripples himself or herself with some sort of fleshly sense of inferiority.

Finally, this church is a many-splendored fellowship because of a great-hearted sense of generosity that Paul enjoins upon us. "Let those who are taught in the word share in all good things with those who teach." One of the noblest figures in John Bunyan's *Pilgrim's Progress*, to me, is Mr. Great-heart. Here was no measly-minded person. Here was no stingy soul. Here was a person who in the pilgrim way saw it as his calling to undergird, to encourage, to lift up, to be magnanimous of heart toward all he met.

I recall a fellowship like this that happened once in the seminary dormitory room of a very sick student whom I had been asked to visit. I visited him and I said to him, "Look, my good friend, you are ill and you need a physician. Will you let me go with you to see a physician? You can be well." And he wouldn't. "No, get out!" he said. I said, "I will get out, but first I must tell you that I must call your father and mother and tell them that you are ill and ask them to come and help us." He didn't object.

I shall never forget what happened when that father came to see his son. He was a farmer from rural Kentucky. He and I went to his son's room. He sat down by his son and put his arm around him. He laid his calloused hand upon him and said, "Son, your pa is here. The good doctor tells me that you are sick and that you need to go see a physician. You must remember, son, that you are our'n and we are your'n." That is the way it is—you are our'n and we are your'n. (Which being translated means you are ours and we are yours!) He said, "Now I want you to get up and put your clothes on because we are going to the doctor." The son got up and put his clothes on and we took him to the doctor, and the doctor got him well. What a difference that father made! He had a greatness of heart toward his son. You are ours and we are yours.

That is what God is saying to us in this many-splendored fellowship of the St. Matthews Baptist Church. You are mine, and in Jesus Christ I bought you with a price, and I am yours. God is a spendthrift with his love. He calls upon us for a greatness of heart. In one of his poems, Sidney Lanier wrote of seeing the marsh hens fly out of the marshes on the South Carolina coast: "By so many roots as the marsh grass sends into the sod I will heartily lay me a-hold of the greatness of God." On this November day, as the people of God, in the many-splendored fellowship of the church at St. Matthews, let us lay a-hold of the greatness of God. It is into this fellowship that we invite you. We commit ourselves to you to be the kind of fellowship that is a fault-bearing, a self-examining, a burden-bearing, a transformed working fellowship to show unto you the greatness of God in this place.

The Community of Faith, Comfort, and Ministry

2 Corinthians 1:3-7

Preached at St. Matthews Baptist Church, Louisville, Kentucky, August 16, 1992

The sermon I have today focuses on the large number of senior adults in our church and in our nation. This is the fastest-growing segment of our population. By the year 2020, the typical family will consist of at least four generations—great-grandparents, grandparents, parents, and children. However, when I say that we are going to talk together about the senior adults in our congregation, that picks up everybody else in the congregation, because we senior adults are grandparents of little children and teenagers. We are aging parents who agonize over the chaos in the families of our married sons and daughters with children, especially adolescents. There are people in our church who are in their fifties and sixties caring for disabled older parents who are in their eighties and nineties in the home or in the nursing homes. So we are all in this boat together in a community of faith, a community of comfort, and a community of ministry.

In a lighter vein, the age sixty-five does not tell us when we are really old. Our symptoms, our disabilities, our behaviors, and our eccentricities do. For example, you are really old when you stop saying, "While you are up, will you get this for me?" and you start saying, "While you are down, will you pick that up for me?" You are not old when you absentmindedly put the telephone book in the refrigerator instead of the cabinet beside it. A mother of three young children can do that! She thinks she is losing her mind. You are not really old until you make a habit of placing the telephone book in the refrigerator and start demanding that the rest of the family do likewise. That is when you are old. Then pain has a way of telling you when you are old, especially pain that has decided not to go away. I awakened the other morning and had no pain at all anywhere. I didn't think I was younger; I thought I was dead! The presence of pain lets me know that I am still alive!

Seriously, we know that we are old when we think that life is over for us, when we have lost curiosity, a sense of adventure, and interest in the people around us. Then we are old. We can become old at any age when that happens. I am grateful for St. Matthews Baptist Church because I don't know of a more close-knit ministering group of people than I find here. Older people being supported and sustained by young people, and young people being guided and inspired by older people. So let's read our Scripture together again. I'll just read verses 3-7 at this time: "Blessed be the God and Father of our Lord Jesus Christ and the father of mercies and all comfort . . . ." That is the community of faith. ". . . who comforts us in all our afflictions." That is the community of comfort. ". . . so that we may be able to comfort those who are in any affliction with which we ourselves are comforted of God." That is the community of ministry.

Let's take those one at a time.

The community of faith in God. Yes. But not just any ordinary old god. Not just any god. Our God is a God above all gods, the Lord of lords. This God is the Father of our Lord Jesus Christ. He is not a vengeful storm god who willingly and willy-nilly inflicts suffering upon us. This God visited us in our human form and suffered temptation, pain, crucifixion, and the opening of the gates of a new life for us. He is the God and Father of our Lord Jesus Christ, the Father of mercies, and the God of all comfort. That word "comfort" comes from the same word from which the name of the Holy Spirit comes. The Comforter, the Counselor, the Paraclete, the One who is called alongside us—not over against us. He is our companion in suffering with whom we can converse and who never leaves us in our loneliness. Suffering isolates you and makes you lonely. The Holy Spirit comes to us and lets us know that God is with us and that we are not alone. He never comes over against us in condemnation but always comes alongside us in comfort and companionship and in conversation. That is the kind of God we have. That is the God we place our faith in and the God who draws us together here on Sunday morning and Sunday evening. That is the God of love and of mercy and of comfort who comforts us in all our afflictions.

In Robert Browning's long poem *Saul*, David, who is ministering to Saul in his depression and who is his healer of despair and loneliness, says to Saul,

> He who did most, shall bear most; the strongest shall stand the most weak.
> 'Tis the weakness in strength, that I cry for! my flesh that I seek
> In the Godhead! I seek and I find it. O Saul, it shall be
> A face like my face that receives thee; a Man like to me,
> Thou shalt love and be loved by, for ever: a Hand like this hand
> Shall throw open the gates of life to thee! See the Christ stand!"[1]

That is our God. That is the community of faith that brought us here this morning, and our faith in this Christ/God who is Jesus lays a hand like my hand upon us to comfort us. A man like me whom we can love and be loved by forever. This is the community of faith of the God of all comfort.

Now, let's look at the community of comfort. This leads us to the second part of the text. This Christ-like God comforts us in all our afflictions. God comes alongside us in all our afflictions. This God does not pick out a favorite few of sufferers. He said, "In any affliction," be it massive business failure, a divorce, cancer, perpetual pain, Alzheimer's disease, Parkinson's, a broken hip that won't mend, AIDS. God is no respecter of people nor is he any respecter of their diseases or calamities. Suffering is no respecter of people either. Some maladies isolate us from people more than others, such as chronic schizophrenia. But, as has been said, all human beings are more alike than they are otherwise. As William James said, "There is very little difference between us human beings. But what little there is we make an awful lot of." We are more alike than we are different. Thus God, the God of all comfort, makes us a community of comfort in any of our afflictions.

Now the third community—the community of ministry. God does not comfort us without a purpose. He does so that we may be enabled to comfort each other by means of the comfort with which he has comforted us. We learn from our sufferings. As Jesus, as it is said in the Scripture, learned obedience from the things that he suffered, we learn obedience and discipline from the things that we suffer. This becomes a set of tools for us as we grow sensitive and compassionate for all people who are suffering. Whatever that suffering is, we become a community of comfort. The main meaning or purpose of suffering is to find a new purpose in life. I don't know of any better explanation of why people suffer than that we might become a comfort to those who are in affliction.

We older people have many, many sufferings. We face, first of all, the suffering of retirement from meaningful work. Then we face the issue of rebuilding a whole new system of habits and rituals and customs whereby our lives will be meaningful. We face the issues of increasing disabilities of body and of mind. We face the possibilities of falling and breaking a hip or an arm such as a dear old friend and teacher of mine did two weeks ago. His birthday came up, and I always call him on his birthday because he was my teacher and my friend. He was nine years older than I, but he became my mentor and my friend. I have copied much of my style of teaching and preaching and ministry from him. I thought he was on vacation. I tried to call him but he was not there. I hoped as I wrote him a letter that he would be having a nice family gathering with his two daughters and their families. But then I got a call from his wife who said that he had fallen and broken a hip and an arm and was in the nursing home. These are just a few of the sufferings that older people face. But it is not just aged people.

This is just the dark side of aging. The bright side comes in the message of the prophet Joel. In Joel 2:28 (and repeated by the Apostle Peter in Acts 2:17), it says, "I will pour out my spirit upon all flesh, and your sons and daughters shall prophesy; your young people shall see visions; and your old people shall dream dreams." The bright side of being older is that we can mingle our dreams with the visions of people younger than we are, and we can cease to compete with younger people and become those who inspire them and who mingle our dreams with their visions so that they will be able to accomplish what we are no longer able to accomplish. We can become their sustaining grace as they do the work of the Lord.

Then, too, there is our role as grandparents. Bill Clinton told of his father having been killed in an automobile accident just before he was born. Then, as a wee lad, he had to be cared for by his grandmother and grandfather while his mother equipped herself to take care of him and to be a nurse. Then his stepfather, whom she had married, became a severe alcoholic and was brutal to him. But the sustaining power in Bill Clinton's life was his grandfather. His grandfather became the tower of strength in the skipping of a generation. In his acceptance speech as president, Clinton said, "I want you to know my grandfather." We, as grandparents, often have to reach past inadequate sons or daughters to get to the needs of our grandchildren. That is one of the heaviest responsibilities a person can possibly have. The community of the congregation is one in which visions and dreams all mingle together across generational lines in order to provide sound, non-exploitative, non-brutal friendship in our relationships to younger people.

I remember well when I was sixty years of age. I had a mother and father of a fifteen-year-old bring their daughter to see me. She was having a great deal of trouble. She came in and sat down in my study. She was in her blue jeans, and she crossed her legs in her chair and "butterflied" her knees and legs. I greeted her and thanked her for coming to see me. She said, "Well, I have one question I want to ask you." I said, "Ask on, Marsha." She said, "Why is it that an old man like you is wasting their time talking to a young squirt like me?" I said, "That is a good question. Let me think on it." I thought a little while then said, "Marsha, you are fifteen and I am sixty, and I am four times older than you. But when I am ninety, and I plan to be ninety with God helping me, you will be forty-five and I won't be but twice as old as you are," and I grinned. "But then I will need you to come to see me because I will be an old man and people will quit coming to see me. I need all the friends your age I can get." She leaned back and said, "Old man, you are something else!" We were friends.

I had a call yesterday from a person whom I had met when she was ten years old. Her father had killed himself with a pistol in the bathroom. She came home from school and found him. I followed this shattered young girl for four or five years. For the first year, every afternoon at five-thirty, I either stopped by her house for a minute, called her on the telephone, or, if I was in a plane somewhere, I wrote her a note and said, "It is five-thirty. I am here and I wanted you to know that you are not alone." She is thirty-three now, and yesterday afternoon we got a call and she and her mother came to see us. It was a bit of ecstasy to see her grown and effective as a social worker in Seattle.

The church is a community of ministry. We search through our congregation and include other people, and we reach out to other people who never darken the door of a church and minister to them in their sufferings and become a comfort to them. This is the meaning of the gospel—a community of faith, a community of comfort, and a community of ministry. God help us.

Note

1. Robert Browning, *Saul*, in *The Complete Works of Robert Browning*, vol. 4, ed. Charlotte Porter and Helen A. Clarke (New York: George D. Sproul, 1898) 85; pt. 103, lines 70–75 (http://www.bartleby.com/236/103.html).

What Do You Say to Yourself?

Luke 12:13-21; 15:17-19; John 16:32

Preached at St. Matthews Baptist Church, Louisville, Kentucky, August 3, 1991

I'm going to be frank with you at the outset of this sermon that nothing I say here will be nearly as important as what you say to yourself. We as human beings have a remarkable capacity to carry on a conversation with ourselves. I am going to drag out an antique joke of the two men who rode the bus to work regularly and sat by each other. One of them talked aloud to himself. Finally, his coworker asked him, "I want to ask you a question. Why is it that you talk to yourself?" He said, "I have two reasons. One is that I like to talk to an intelligent man, and the other one is I like to hear an intelligent man talk." So in our conversations with ourselves, our real opinion of who we think we are comes out.

Children are aware of this ability very early. I recall our oldest son when he was three years old learning how to use the two words "shut up" at the most inopportune moments. Guests would come to our apartment, and he would in the middle of dinner say to them, "Shut up!" It got to be awfully bad when, instead of telling them goodbye, he would tell them to shut up. I was put, and his mother was put, into the position of telling Bill to shut up saying shut up! He did when I finally drew the line and said, "No more of this nonsense! We don't want you ever to say 'shut up' to anybody who is talking. Even if you feel like it, don't say it!" Well, it went on for about two weeks and he was a model child. He never said it. I was driving in the car with him one day and he was on the back seat. He began to laugh to himself. I said, "What's funny, Bill?" He said, "Daddy, I just found that I can say 'shut up' to myself and nobody minds!" We have this capacity to talk to ourselves.

I recall how it came to me in the second grade on a playground. I was watching the other children play. I suddenly discovered that I could watch my own mind, that I could say something to myself. At no time in my waking hours was I not thinking and talking to myself about what was going on around me. It has been a treasure to me all these years ever since. I have built upon it until I have an elaborate superstructure of conversations with myself. Children learn this early. Sometimes it is not just you talking to yourself or me talking to my "me." Quite often there is a crowd within us. There seems to be more than one self there, contrary with one another. There is a bit of doggerel poetry that says it well:

Within this earthly temple there is a crowd.
There is one of me that is humble and one of me that is proud.
There is one of me that is sorry for his sins,
And there is one of me that unrepentant sits and grins.
From much undue anxiety I would be free.
If I could once decide which of these is me.[1]

The Scriptures that we read give us three brilliant pictures of biblical characters who talked to themselves. The Bible is replete with private conversations of the self with the self. I'll just pick out three.

The one I first read is of the rich fool who became so affluent that he didn't know what to do with his possessions. He decided to tear down his barns and build bigger ones. Then he said to himself, "So you have much goods laid up for years to come. Take it easy. Relax, enjoy yourself. Eat, drink, and be merry." But another thing about the conversations that we have with ourselves is that we are not in there alone. The Spirit of the Living God is hearing our conversation. God spoke up and said, "You fool!" Now, I'll be candid with you. I would much rather be called a sinner than a fool. There is some sort of red-blooded macho spirit that goes into straightforward, honest sin. To be called a fool, a person with no mind, is a put-down. "Thou fool. This night your very life will be required of you. You will be dead. Then whose will these be?" The answer to that question is in the context. Jesus told this story when a young man came to him and asked that his father's inheritance be divided between him and his brother. Well, whose will they be when the brothers are gone? They will be other people's to fuss and fight over.

Some of the most vicious parts of the grief process of losing someone by death is the way people fight with one another over practically nothing in the inheritance. I have led funerals and have comforted people through the deaths of their loved ones. Then hell on earth breaks loose, and these people become less than human with each other. "Then whose will these things be?" Well, this man was a relatively honest fool. He had some concrete things in mind for his foolish conversation with himself. He was a materialist. He was self-absorbed.

But look at another occasion in Luke 18 where the Pharisee stands and prays to God and thanks God that "I am not like other people—extortionists, adulterers, unjust, or even this tax collector. I fast twice a week and I give tithes of all I get." The truth is that the Pharisee prayed thus within himself. His prayers were conversations with himself and not with God. But the prayer of self-confrontation was that of the publican: "God, have mercy on me, a sinner."

That takes us to the second Scripture—the prodigal son. He had many friends around him as long as he had money. But he wasted his substance in foolish living. A famine came and he had nothing. He hired himself out to a swine keeper. That was a dirty, nasty job for anybody, but it was especially so for a Jew because they don't like pork. They think it is unclean. He was hungry and had hit bottom, and he began to talk to himself. He said, "How many of my father's servants have food to eat and to spare and here I languish in hunger?" Then he said, when he came to himself, "I will go to my father and I will say to him, 'Father, I have sinned against heaven and in thy sight.'" He made a hundred and eighty degree turnaround of his life in that conversation with himself.

We often think of conversion as some sort of inward/outward/all-over feeling of the holy glow of what Dr. Dobbins used to call "holy moonshine." But conversion, in the New Testament, means to turn around a hundred and eighty degrees and change your direction in life. You may have come here this morning in despair over the direction that your life is taking. I hope now, at this very moment, you are beginning to say to yourself, "I am going to turn around and change the direction and course of my life. I am going to let all the people of God hear and know that I am doing that. I am going to make a profession of my faith in the Lord Jesus Christ, and whereas I have been going in this direction, I will turn and go in his direction."

Conversion is the matter of the direction in which your life is going and how you plan to turn out in the long run. Or, as older people often say, "I don't know what on earth is ever going to become of that person." What are you going to become in the long run? I hope you are talking to yourself about that. This is a conversation with one's self in which self-confrontation takes place. Nobody had to tell the prodigal son what he should do. He told himself.

The third story of someone talking to himself is found in John 16:32 in which Jesus is talking to his disciples and he says, "The time is come, the hour has come." In the book of John, that is a rhythmic passage. It starts out, "Mine hour has not yet come. Mine hour has not yet come." Then, on this occasion in John 16, he says, "My hour is at hand"—the hour of his crucifixion, of his death on the cross for you and me. He said to his disciples, "You will each one go your own way and abandon me. But I will not be alone, for my Father in heaven is with me." Loneliness is what he experienced. Even on the cross he said, "My God, my God, why have thou forsaken me?" He felt lonely. I don't know of any more prevalent feeling than the feeling of loneliness in people's hearts. I must carry this myself. I can't tell anybody about this. Nobody would care if I did. I am alone, as Coleridge's Ancient Mariner said, "Alone, alone, all alone with never a soul to take pity on me and my agony."

You may be experiencing a deep kind of loneliness today. The promise of Jesus the Christ is this: "I will not have you as orphans. I and my Father will come to you in the Holy Spirit and make our home with you. You will never be alone again, for I will be with you to comfort you." The opposite of loneliness is the formation of a community of faith. St. Matthews Baptist Church has formed a community of faith that we might not be alone, that each of us would have some of us as a support system to go through things with us that we might not be alone. You have gone through things with me and I have felt, and Pauline has felt, the encircling community of your companionship as we went through them together. That is the invitation that this church offers anyone here—an invitation to a community of faith, of people who believe in each other, of people who trust each other, of people who believe in the Lord Jesus Christ and bring our lives under the scrutiny of his will. We open up our private conversations with ourselves to his inspection and ask for his approval. That is what you have here in this place and among these people.

Note

1. Edward Sanford Martin, "My Name Is Legion." This poem can be found in various versions online.

10

Flying, Running, Walking

Isaiah 40:28-31; Matthew 11:27-30

Preached at St. Matthews Baptist Church, Louisville, Kentucky, August 6, 1989

When we read the Scripture, we need to know to whom it was originally addressed and what the author had in mind behind the words. That is especially true of our reading of Isaiah 40:28 and following. Now to bring that statement somewhat more closely to home, let me think of this passage with you as if it were a letter. You read the addresses on your mail when you pick it up each day. Somebody went to the trouble and cost to send something that landed in your mailbox. But when you start separating that mail you may find those dear letters addressed to your name in the handwriting of someone else. There is nothing quite as warm and deep as a handwritten letter. We are losing this art today when we pick up the telephone instead of writing. But remember that when we write a letter, a person can read it again over and over. So that is very special.

On the other hand, then you find one in thorough business fashion that has your name typed individually on the envelope itself and you say, "Oh, my goodness! It is a bill." Or "It is an official document of some kind." And you put up with it. But then your ire begins to rise a little bit when the letter you get has your name on a computer sticker. Somebody has cranked and turned your name out on a computer and put it on your mail. But the insult above all insults is the letter that simply says, "Occupant!" 3500 Winchester Road. "Occupant." That is not very personal, is it?

Regardless of appearance, you know from whom all of these letters came and you know certainly they came to you. Reading the Scripture requires knowing to whom it was addressed, its time in history, and the circumstances surrounding it. Who then was the audience of this stellar passage that we read again and again and memorize and comfort ourselves with? When we are exhausted, when we are tired, and when we have "had it," we read this passage and are strengthened by it. This passage, from all that I can learn, was addressed to a group of Jews in exile in Babylon. The first of them had been carried away in 534–539 BC. The temple had been destroyed and Jerusalem had been smashed and they were carried away as captives. Psalm 137 says,

> By the waters of Babylon, there we sat down and wept, when we remembered Zion. On the willows there we hung up our harps. For there our captors required of us songs, and our tormentors, mirth, saying, "Sing us one of the songs of Zion." But how shall we sing the LORD's song in a foreign land? If I forget you, O Jerusalem, let my right hand wither! Let my tongue cleave to the roof of my mouth, if I do not remember you, if I do not set Jerusalem above my highest joy!

They had been captured in three groups that amounted to nearly or over four thousand people. There they were stuck as captives in the land of Babylon. The Babylonians gave them a good deal of freedom, and they broke up into about three different groups. There were those who despaired of the Lord God Jehovah and felt that he had let them down. They had believed in him but now he had been so careless of them that he had let them down. So they blended into the woodwork of the worship of the great god Marduk, the idol of the Babylonians. Then there was the group who held strongly to the hope of a return someday of Zion, and they continued to sing songs like I have read to you from Psalm 137. Then there was that group who was born there, who had never known Jerusalem and wondered what it was all about. They grew up in Babylon. Because, after all, the group that had been there the longest were there fifty-nine years. That is, those of them who had not died. The other groups had been there forty-eight years and forty-three years, respectively. Here was this third group who had never known Jerusalem except as they heard about it from their parents. These three groups were there when this passage was written.

In this passage, they had been called to make the journey back to Jerusalem and to rebuild the city and the temple. Some of them were living on borrowed time—that is, if they were living and not already dead. They were very young when they were deported, fifty-nine, forty-eight, and forty-three years ago. The Lord called unto them that they should go back to Jerusalem and he spoke these words: "Comfort ye, comfort ye my people, says your God. Speak tenderly to Jerusalem, and cry to her that her warfare is ended, that her iniquity is pardoned, that she has received from the LORD's hand double for all her sins." A voice cries, "In the wilderness prepare the way of the LORD, make straight in the desert a highway for our God. Every valley shall be lifted up, and every mountain and hill be made low; the uneven ground shall become level, and the rough places a plain. And the glory of the LORD shall be revealed, and all flesh shall see it together, for the mouth of the LORD has spoken."

Who was to be the agent of this deliverance? Cyrus of Assyria. He is the one whom God had appointed as his own shepherd and in one place he appoints him as his anointed, a noun that can be translated "his messiah." Cyrus the Assyrian, as I am told by my esteemed colleague, Dr. Smothers, was the only person in the Old Testament to receive the name "messiah." He was the hand of God outstretched to deliver his people once again from their captivity in Babylon. Cyrus did that, and they began to get ready. They were a lot like the congregation of St. Matthews. They were senior citizens, if they were lucky to have lived beyond their three score and ten, having come young to the land.

There were those who were middle-aged adults in their forties and fifties, maybe in their early sixties. Then there were all those young people who had never been to Jerusalem. God said to them, "The LORD is the everlasting God, the creator of the ends of the earth. He does not grow faint or weary. His understanding is unsearchable. He gives power to the faint." There were those who were faint-hearted, wondering, "What is the use? Can we make it in a long trek across the desert and to rebuild the temple in Jerusalem? We don't have the strength for that." The Lord said, "He gives power to the faint, and to him who has no might he increases strength." There is a reference here: "Even the youth shall faint and be weary; and the young person shall fall exhausted. But they who wait for the LORD shall renew their strength." Then he makes promises to them. Some were so elated and filled with enthusiasm and joy; I imagine that they were filled with such anticipation for the liberation of Cyrus that they felt like they could fly to Jerusalem.

Have you ever wanted to be somewhere and thought it would be great to get there by magic? The worst thing about being somewhere else is how much energy it takes to get there. One thing you would have to do is travel. Then you would say to yourself, "No, thanks. It is the getting there that is the problem." Especially with airline strikes and anxiety about the age of the airplane that you are on. Yes, it would be great just to be there in Jerusalem. But we have got to make that long trek. The Lord says, "They that wait upon the LORD shall renew their strength." What does "wait" mean? It means passively that we are steady, that we are remaining, that we are standing, and, having stood all, we are standing again, waiting for direction from God. In good east Kentucky language, it would mean that we are standing "hitched," ready to go. But we are not going to run ahead of God. It has a deeper meaning than that. It has a meaning of expectation; of looking forward to; of hope.

These exiles had a demanding journey before them. At first their energy would be so great that, with God's help, they could—figuratively speaking—fly like eagles. As the distance increased, they could run and not be weary. As they got further, they could walk and not faint. Yet all these were energized as they waited patiently on the Lord. His presence, his purpose, and his power energized the whole journey. Without it, even the young people would faint and utterly fall.

This passage reminds me of the situation we now have at St. Matthews as we get ready once again to raise funds to pay for this temple to God. We acknowledge that it was by God's strength, who helped us to rebuild, that we have our building today. I don't know how they financed the business, but I imagine Cyrus helped pay the bills. Well, we certainly have no Cyrus when we start a third fundraising campaign to pay off the indebtedness of this building. One of the feelings I got when I read the St. Matthews Baptist newsletter was that the congregation, of which Pauline and I are a part—we realized that we were flying to begin with. The "Together We Build" campaign was easy then because we weren't even in our temple at that point. We were at the seminary and other places all over St. Matthews. In the "Together We Share" campaign, we said, "Of course, of course, we have got to carry this on." We were running. That was in 1986, the year after we moved in here. But now it's 1989! We are down to the walking stage. This is getting a little tiresome. This is beginning to get to me. Now, if you don't have those feelings, count yourself out. But if, on examining your heart, you do have those feelings, count yourself in. I was amazed to see a change that took place when the committee first decided to name this fundraising drive. The name they thought of was "We Can Make It Happen." But they were not comfortable with that. It seemed that it was a bootstrap operation, that in our own strength we can make it. I suppose if we tithed and did a good deal more, we could raise the funds without trying too hard. But they were uncomfortable with that name and asked for suggestions as to a better one. A better one came from a member of the congregation. It was agreed that this effort would be called "With God We Can." I am calling on us as a congregation who may be faint and need strength to wait before God. As you make your pledge, ask God for strength, expect of God that God will give you strength, and hope in God that your life will be renewed in the process of your giving.

You thought I was through, didn't you? I have only told you half of the story. If we do what I have suggested we do, we are still in the throes of a severe temptation of making this building, or these buildings, our idea of what church is. The Jews had done that by the time Jesus got to them in the third decade of the first century. They were hogtied and loaded down with the weight of the law and the practices of the temple. The temple had become their religion. Jesus came preaching. Jesus saw them under that load. The Pharisees had bound heavy burdens upon the people of God and did not even lift one finger to help bear them. Their individual load and burden of the law was too much. It was then that Jesus said, "Come unto me all you who labor and are heavy laden and I will cause you to rest. Take my yoke upon you for my yoke is easy, and my burden is light." This is the Messiah who did not have anywhere to lay his head, who spoke in the marketplace, who was not above or beyond worshiping in a synagogue, but who knew in his heart that neither the temple nor the synagogue was where the action was. He saw people carrying all sorts of burdens that were heavier than they knew what to do with. In this congregation today, there would be hardly a family that is not confronting difficulties, temptations, or burdens. There would hardly be a person who does not need to come unto the Lord Jesus and take his yoke upon you, for that yoke is easy and that burden is light.

11

The Daily Providence of God

Exodus 16:4-6, 11-21; Matthew 6:11, 34

Preached at St. Matthews Baptist Church, Louisville, Kentucky, June 24, 1984

Sir William Osler was one of the outstanding pioneer physicians in modern American medicine. On one occasion, he was making a journey to Europe by ship. An accident occurred. Their ship was hit by another ship. The bow of the other ship pierced a hole in the side of their ship. Everyone was filled with anxiety, terrified. But the crew calmed them, saying, "We have the situation in hand. It is under control." Sir William found out later that the way they had it under control was due to the way the ship had been built in the first place. If it sustained this kind of damage, watertight sealed doors could be closed around the one hole. Then they could carry a certain amount of water with them and make it to port safely for repair.

This wise man began to think about what had happened. Providence had come to those travelers from God. On the rest of that journey, he wrote a little essay titled "A Way of Life." He used the closing off of a portion of the ship to set forth a way of life that he called "living life in day tight compartments." If one of your days is completely sabotaged, this too will pass. "Sufficient unto the day are the troubles thereof"—he took that as his text. Upon reading this book, I was reminded of the story of the children of Israel as they made their journey from the Red Sea into the promised land. They got more and more impatient with Moses. They expressed their anger more and more to him because they did not have the kind of food they had had when they were in bondage in Egypt. The Lord said to them through Moses, "I will give you manna in the morning; when the dew has risen you will find it. And in the evening I will give you meat, and quails will come in the evening. And in the evening you will have meat. And then you shall know that I am God." It is not meat, not bread, not the enemy, I am God.

This is the main issue in our life today: how to live with foresight and planning and at the same time to the utmost for God. How can you and I perceive our spiritual life as a long journey, invest our lives with confidence in this day for the future? At the same time, how can we not live in the past or live in the future in such a way that the present day is totally wasted in anxiety over the future and guilt over the past? That is the issue that I want to address in our understanding of the daily providence of God.

I will enter a disclaimer with you at the outset and say, yes, the Scripture also teaches the other side of this coin, namely that we are to invest our lives providently in behalf of the future, that we are to invest it with good stewardship today in behalf of our future, that we are not to be wicked and unprofitable servants who hold back our commitment and make no thought of the morrow at all. No. Each of us is to use his or her talents in this day in such a way that the days to follow will not be days of regret and remorse. Anybody who wants tulips in May had better not say so in May unless they have planted bulbs in November. These are companion truths. When we consecrate our attention on the fullest expression of our lives today, tomorrow will take care of itself, so Jesus tells us.

God speaks to us about different kinds of days that we have. There is a day of desire. There is a day of difficulty. There is a day of decision. In the day of desire, God saves us from the idolatry of our desire. The Israelites had thrown a tantrum with God. They remind me, and we remind me, of myself and yourself too, of the impatience of the grandchild of a good friend of mine who came to him and said, "Grandpa, I want this right now. I want it right in the middle of now." When we want, when we desire, we want right in the middle of now. That is our impatience. That is our hunger. I can recall our oldest son on one occasion asking me for something. I said, "Well, be patient son, and you will get it when you least are expecting it." He said "okay" and went out. In about five minutes he came back and said, "Daddy." I said, "Yes, son." He said, "I am least expecting it now!"

The Israelites went one step further. They not only expected it now but they also expected to have a surplus so they wouldn't have to depend on God later. When we start building our surpluses out of keeping with reality, this becomes greed and an idolatry of our desires. Jesus said, "Give us this day our daily bread." But the greed we are tempted by is like that of a man whom I visited in the hospital during World War II. He was in a tubercular sanitarium at Waverly Hills. He was a man who worked with his hands. As I visited him, I said to him, "Well, tell me how it is with you. I want to know how things are with you." He said, "I wouldn't be here if it weren't for my sin." I said, "Sin? What did you do?" He said, "Well, I wanted it all. The ammunition plant across the river was short of help and the wages were high. All of the men were in the war. I got a job there and could work as many shifts of overtime as I wanted to work. Many times I wouldn't sleep over twelve, fourteen, sixteen hours in a week. I worked because I wanted it all. Then the Lord made me lie down, and that's why I'm here. I wanted it all." There is a difference in planning for the future by tending to the well-being of those whom we love and in wanting it all. There is a difference between foresight and an idolatry of the surplus. In the dew of each morning's need for material necessities comes bread. In the evening of that day comes meat. Then we know that God, and not our desire, is God.

The day of difficulty comes and God provides us with the strength and wisdom for resolving our difficulties on a day-by-day basis. Jesus, in addressing the anxiety of our heart, says, "Do not be anxious for the morrow; let tomorrow be anxious for itself." There is a difference between wise planning and being overwhelmed by anxiety. He said sufficient unto the day is the evil thereof. Suffering and loss come upon us. We lose loved ones. We feel that we cannot go on another day. We feel that we have had it. We may not be able to go on another day, but we can go on this day. God provides the strength for this day. There is no stress or temptation that has overcome us that God won't provide a way through it. This is so we may know that he is God.

Alcoholics Anonymous is an excellent example of this. If you ask a tried and true member of AA if he or she is free of the temptation to drink, he or she will tell you no. "Only for today. I am dry twenty-four hours at a time." Through this discipline, AA has had better fruits of their efforts in removing people from the habit of alcoholism than any other way of treating them. Yes, there are other habits too. There is the habit of uncontrollable anger and temper. Those who know me best know that if I should be pointing the finger at any one of you on this, three more would be pointing back at me. The maintenance of control over one's impatience and wrath is a day-by-day discipline. Paul put it well when he said in Ephesians 4:25, "Therefore putting away falsehood, let everyone speak the truth with his neighbor, for we are members one of another. Be angry and sin not and do not let the sun go down on your wrath or give opportunity to the devil." So, as in eating, to control one's anger is a habit that can replace the tantrums the children of Israel expressed. They, and you and I, learn to discipline anger day by day. We learn to put that energy into constructive activity day by day and make it produce British thermal units of energy for work to the glory of the Lord. Jesus said, "Agree with your adversary quickly while you are in the way with him. For you will in no wise get out until you pay the last farthing." The accumulation of unresolved habits that are destructive to us becomes heavier and heavier. It becomes a burdensome way of life. Our angers and our grudges become little gods before whom we bow down and worship. But when, day by day, we get angry and yet sin not, God becomes our God rather than our grudges being our god.

Finally comes the day of decision. God provides us light, love, and strength to make decisions every day. Jesus said to Zacchaeus in the nineteenth chapter of Luke, "Today salvation has come to this house." Zacchaeus brought his desires, difficulties, and decisions in eager hospitality to Jesus' entry into his life. Basic changes took place. A clear decision was made to follow the Christ. As we face the decisions about our lives, we decide whether we are going to serve God or the gods around us, as Joshua had to ask the Israelites on another occasion. We are faced with the temptation of procrastination—putting things off day by day; letting decisions go unmade until they are made for us by the passage of time. This is no plea for impulsive lack of thought through decisions, because wisdom is justified of its children. It is a plea for the more common ailment we suffer, procrastination, to come to an end. I know people who have thought for years, "I will give my life to Jesus Christ someday. I will make a 180-degree turnaround in my life someday, but not today. I'm afraid of that responsibility. I'm afraid I may not be able to hold out." Faith in God is a candle put into our hands by God through Jesus Christ.

If we have the courage to take the step today on behalf of our commitment to Jesus Christ, his promise is that we will have the light to take the step tomorrow. Minnie Louise Haskins wrote a poignantly beautiful comment: "I said to the man at the gate of the year; Give me a light that I may tread safely into the unknown. But he said unto me, Go out into the darkness. Place your hand in the hand of the Lord. That will be to you better than a light and safer than the known way."

The Struggle for Maturity

1 Corinthians 13:11; Hebrews 6:1-2; Ephesians 4:13-16

Preached in a number of places including First Baptist, Lumberton, North Carolina, and published in The Revelation of God in Human Suffering[1]

The struggle for maturity entails more suffering than most of our momentary afflictions. Our capacity to learn from them, to discern the workings of the mind of God in stressful situations, and to take hold of the maturing resources of God's grace in these momentary situations largely depends on our accrued maturity in Christ. The struggle for maturity is, at the heart of its meaning, the thrust of the total person in the ceaselessly changing and growing experience of relating oneself abidingly to other people and to God. The process of building mature relationships to God and to our community is another way of saying that through the divine gift of God's love, we are initially enabled to begin to participate in the kingdom of God. God lays the foundation of the building of mature relationships to himself and others by first having loved us in Jesus Christ our Lord. He touches us in our infirmities and quickens us in our incapacities; he perceives our low estimates of ourselves and discerns the impediments of our character that hinder us from loving him and one another with abandon and wholehearted passion, unsullied by lust. Mature relationships do not happen when we lift ourselves by the bootstraps of self-effort. Mature relationships are activated out of the heart of God who valued us in a way we could never have valued ourselves: he so loved us that he gave himself for us.

The love of God as the beginning and end of mature relationships is set forth in the thirteenth chapter of 1 Corinthians. Here the perfect love of God, the necessity for mature relationships to God and to one another, and the different kinds of immaturity among growing Christians are all set forth.

First, let us look at the different kinds of immaturity among growing Christians. Second, the supreme criterion of spiritual maturity, love, as the heart of interpersonal relationships needs consideration. Finally, the practical ways in which this maturity expresses itself in interpersonal living will be given attention.

The Christian, having encountered the love of God and having entered the Christian life, is, nevertheless, still involved in spiritual immaturities of various kinds. The "if's" of 1 Corinthians 13:1-3 depict four types of spiritual immaturity.

Spiritual Articulation. The first immaturity is the stage of spiritual growth I choose to call the articulation and explanation of the remarkable change that has occurred in one's inner being. The early Christians, like many of us, were often uneducated and unlettered people when they entered the Christian life. They could not find words to describe their feelings. The message of the new being in Christ burned within them and sought expression in words lest it consume them with its intensity. Some of them were so overcome with its power that they could only babble like an infant. They burst forth in unknown tongues, with no language but a cry. Yet others who also had become Christians could understand through subverbal communication what their spiritual kinsmen were trying to utter. Paul cautioned his converts, however, to work at the business of making themselves clearly understood, lest outsiders and unbelievers consider them mad. Five words with a clear understanding are more instructive than ten thousand words in a tongue (see 1 Cor 14:24 and 19, respectively).

Men like Apollos were eloquent and spoke with much smoothness and power of oratory. Paul saw "cliques" of Christians go off after Apollos and was quite aware of the fact that he himself did not speak in "lofty words of wisdom" (1 Cor 2: 1). He saw that many of the Corinthian Christians had become fixated at this level of spiritual maturity and were involved in speaking "in the tongues of men and of angels." As they became so fixated, they were more and more immature as time went on.

Even so, you and I get the impression too often that the person who can say his gospel most beautifully is the one most mature. We tend to judge ourselves and others by our ability to speak of the gospel.

Speech is, after all, the lifeline of our communication with one another. It is here that counseling and healing begin: in the articulation of feeling and communication. We must, therefore, never cease to work at the business of devising ways of making ourselves understood to one another. Much of our irritability, our impatience, our rudeness, and our rejoicing when others go wrong comes from our inability to make ourselves understood to others. Our stubborn unwillingness to discipline ourselves to hear what they have to say leads to confused relationships. Rather, we are thinking about what we are going to say instead of listening to them as they talk.

However, our most profound communication is deeper than words and consists of those "groanings of the spirit which cannot be uttered." Just telling their troubles does not necessarily make people whole. Communication must grow apace with the development of our capacity to love. "Even if we speak in the tongues of men and of angels, and have not this, we are as a noisy gong or a clanging cymbal." We have not matured in our love if we stop here in our growth. If many of us like this get together, we may develop a "tin-pan alley" religious cult.

Spiritual Understanding. The development of insight and understanding, knowledge, and the sense of mystery is a second type of immaturity. To the psychologically sophisticated, this sounds strange because we tend to equate insight and maturity. But it is only a second way station in the pilgrimage to maturity. The more we try to communicate our experience as Christians, the more it is necessary for us to develop insight and understanding of ourselves and others. We learn how to be self-aware without being self-conscious and uneasy. We learn how to understand our own motivations and those of others without letting our understanding become a tool for our power to condemn ourselves and others. We learn how to be prophetic for the whole mind of God. We learn how to participate in the mysterious presence and ineffable knowledge of God without becoming a cultist or a spiritually arrogant individual.

Paul confronted people among the Corinthians who had lost their balance on these important issues. He confronted the Greek philosophers who had "all knowledge" and often wanted it known. He also confronted the worshipers of the mystery cults of the day. He had to warn his followers of false prophets who had come among them. These people permitted their systems of faith, organizations of knowledge, and particular "in-group" relationships to a few individuals to cut them off and isolate them from the larger Christian community. Apart from the power of love in interpersonal relationships, even knowledge itself becomes a divisive factor.

The reality of these truths is at every hand in the academic world of colleges and universities, seminaries, and divinity schools today. As Robert Frost says in his poem "The Cabin in the Clearing," we live "in the fond faith," where "accumulated fact will of itself take fire and light the world up." As T. S. Eliot has aptly said,

Where is the wisdom we have lost in knowledge?
Where is the knowledge we have lost in information?[2]

Likewise, analytically oriented persons are likely to stop growing at the very point of delving for more and more subtle and occult interpretations of their own motives. Having been given the power to love, they may stop at futile speculation! If we stop in the pilgrimage of our spiritual lives at this plateau, we have not moved to the highest level of maturity in building our relationships to God and others. We must move on. This is no stopping place, only a rest along the way.

The Moving Power of Faith. A third kind of immaturity suggested by Paul is an overdependence on a "moving" faith, demonstrating its power. Overwhelmed by the inadequacy of our knowledge, that is, that we know in part and prophesy in part, we move upward to realize that we live by faith. We begin to "trust in the Lord with all our hearts and lean not on our own understanding." We may even tend to disparage the value of human knowledge and decry the efforts of science. We may discount these realities to such an extent as to set science and religion over against each other. Instead of becoming a minister of reconciliation, we may turn into an apostle of discord. Pushed by our immaturity at this point, we may feel compelled to demonstrate the power of faith, that is, that it can move mountains, help people get well without the aid of doctors, solve our economic distress without the necessity of work, and so on. These signs of immaturity were evident when Paul ministered to the Corinthians, and the timelessness of his truth is obvious in that they are still seen in the realm of those who profess themselves to be the most powerful in faith above all others. Likewise, people who have been in deeper analysis and psychotherapy may avoid adult decisions and impossible action by extolling the virtues of their analyst, of analysis, and of its necessity for "every living creature."

But even here in the demonstration of faith above all others, we can easily see that such "uses" of faith and therapy divide people from one another rather than nurture them in sustaining relationships of love. Paul, in another place (Gal 5:6), says that "faith works through love." In the thirteenth chapter of 1 Corinthians, he tells us that he is as nothing in spiritual apprehension and maturity as long as he uses his faith as a means of gain, that is, to demonstrate his personal prowess.

The Peril of Activism. A fourth type of spiritual immaturity that we encounter on our pilgrimage toward maturity is seen in our attempts to express our faith through a vocation. Here we center on becoming proficient in our work. We become activists who are set to a task and not to be deterred from it. This is good, but it is both our hope and our destruction. Our hope is here because it means that we have a sense of responsibility that motivates us to effective action. Our destruction is here because here lies our capacity to deceive ourselves into believing that the way to relate ourselves to God is by the sheer results of our work achievements.

We burn the candle at both ends, we "rack up" our successes, we carefully record our achievements, we remind others of our most recent honors, and we keep our right hand informed of what our left hand is doing at all times. Yet the inner gnawing of anxiety tells us that we are missing the main point of living and that we have gained nothing in reality. We have missed the power of the joy that comes to us by having taken the time to establish enduring and satisfying relationships to people and to inquire in the temple of the Lord how we may know and love him better. T. S. Eliot again helps us when he says,

> What life have you if you have not life together?
> There is no life that is not in community,
> And no community not lived in praise of God.
> And now you live dispersed on ribbon roads,
> And no man knows or cares who is his neighbour
> Unless his neighbour makes too much disturbance,
> But all dash to and fro in motor cars,
> Familiar with the roads and settled nowhere . . .
> And the wind shall say: "Here were decent godless people:
> Their only monument the asphalt road
> And a thousand lost golf balls."[3]

This is descriptive of the person today whose profession becomes his religion. He gives up his "body to be burned" in activistic achievement. This is his religion. He may be a doctor, a minister, a social worker, a lawyer, a psychologist, or a scientist in the physical sciences. He reaches the age of thirty-five or forty with a breathless anxiety, burned up with ambition, eaten out with tension, and fearfully apprehensive of his health. He may have the "success syndrome" of ulcers, heart pains, fatigue, confusion, and an inner sense of emptiness, meaninglessness, and boredom. He is a stranger to his family and at cross purposes with his fellow workers, and he feels that he is in a far country, far from God.

All four of these types of immaturity are really way stations along the path toward spiritual maturity in relationship to God and others. They point in the direction of maturity only when we make the supreme criterion of maturity—agape, Christian love—our aim. When we reach this realization, then speaking "in the tongues of men and of angels," developing "prophetic powers" and a moving faith, achieving knowledge and insight, and giving up our bodies to be burned in activistic competition—all these appear at best as ways of establishing relationships of love to God and our fellow man.

The Full-grownness of Love. Therefore, we need to arrive at an understanding of the meaning of love in terms of our maturity in relationship to God and others. In a word, without Christian love, all our other efforts at maturity thrust us into an encounter with nothingness, embroil us in futility, and make of life an empty meaninglessness that threatens our very being. We become as nothing.

Martin Buber gives a concept of interpersonal relationships in his book *I and Thou*, whereby we may think in a straight line about the true maturity in relationship to God and others. He says that there are two kinds of relationships to God and others. The first relationship is the I-It relationship, in which we "use" God and others to achieve our own chosen ends, apart from a free-hearted participation on the part of God and others in our choosing of the ends we would achieve. Such a relationship treats people as things and God as an occult power for our manipulation. It is characterized by an extractive kind of relatedness whereby we get out of people what we want, develop hostile relationships to them, and then no longer have any use for them. As we often say about people we do not like—or better, people we cannot dominate, use, or manipulate—"we don't have a bit of use for them." Naturally, the very image of God within other people rises up in rebellion at such exploitation, and a real break in interpersonal relationships occurs.

Prayer, which is the name we give to our interpersonal relationship to God, can be understood afresh from this point of view. Many people relate themselves to God at one time or another in an I-It kind of prayer. God becomes a "purveyor to their own appetites," to use Robert Browning's phrase, one who caters to their own chosen ends in life, ends that have been chosen without consulting or considering God's creative plan for life. A fervent desire to achieve some chosen end becomes, for all practical purposes, a god, an idol, and the eternal God and Father of our Lord Jesus Christ becomes the servant of the idol—in our own deluded way of thinking, to say the least. As such, prayer becomes a type of magic, that is, the management of infinite powers by finite persons. This is particularly true in the search for health and financial success.

Buber suggests a second kind of relationship that is radically different from the I-It relationship. He calls it the I-Thou relationship. Here we relate ourselves to God and to one another as persons and not as things. Persons are ends within themselves rather than means to ulterior ends. The content of the Christian meaning of love can be put into Buber's concept of the I-Thou relationship, thereby aiding us in a vital discovery of the meaning of the prophetic conception of love that had its roots in Hebrew thinking. Love is the capacity to accept responsibility for others and to relate to them in terms of their essential rather than their instrumental value. People are more than sheep or cattle; they are more than mere measuring sticks for our own ego achievements; they are more than tools for us to exploit. They are essentially valuable in and of themselves as persons for whom Christ died, as having been initially made in the image of God.

Likewise, God is the chief end of our existence, not we the chief end of his being. We find our prayers filled with all the fullness of God when we glorify him rather than attempt to subvert him to our petty pursuits in life. Prayer becomes adoration, thanksgiving, participation in fellowship, and the transformation of our selfhood into the likeness of him more than mere petition and a childish whining after one toy of desire and another. These things are added unto us, not as the end intention but as the "afterthought by-product" of God's already existing knowledge of our needs.

The practical outworking of such a relationship of mature love of God and others is obvious in the thinking of Paul.

When we have mature love, we become more secure and can be freed more and more of our impatience and unkindness toward others. We can evaluate their misunderstandings of us in a new light: the light of our failure to communicate our real motives clearly and in the light of our inhuman use of them as humans. We are not so watchful of self-comparisons because our own status is built by their success. The necessity for arrogance and rudeness is nil in genuinely secure people who feel that they have been accepted and understood for what they are really worth: persons for whom Christ died. Such persons value one another so highly that there is no need to build one another or themselves up through bragging and boasting. They can only rejoice in the success of others and be grieved by others' failures. The relationships of life become more enduring, and they last on.

In the relationships of love, Jesus Christ is always breaking through in some new revelation of his love through persons' concern for one another.

Mature Christians are always searching their relationships to others and testing their knowledge of God with others. They live in the constant hope that God will again make himself known to them in their breaking of bread with one another. Their speaking, their prophecy, their understanding, and their faith and works are all set into a new contextual meaning of the love of God. This love, made known to them in the abiding relationship of Christ to them in the new covenant of his blood, becomes their clear channel of interpersonal relationships to one another.

NOTES

1. Wayne E. Oates, "The Struggle for Maturity," in *The Revelation of God in Human Suffering* (Philadelphia: Westminster Press, 1959) and later republished in *The Preaching Pastor* (St. Louis MO: Bethany Press, 1966) 196–208.

2. From T. S. Eliot, "Choruses from 'The Rock,'" in *Collected Poems 1909–1962* (Harcourt, Brace & World, Inc.). Reprinted by permission.

3. Ibid.

13

How Can We Know the Will of God?

Romans 12:1-2

Man's noblest passion is to know the will of God. As Dante says, "In His will is our peace." How then can we know the will of God? Six down-to-earth suggestions come to us from Jesus himself, who learned by experience what is the good and perfect will of God.

First, *Jesus had faith in God.* To him God was not a theory to be discussed but a Father whose will is to be known and obeyed. Jesus realized that it is men's faith that saves them. Without faith it is impossible to know the will of God. Faith is the stuff of which our hopes are made. It is the convictions we have concerning the things we cannot see and handle. If, therefore, you do not believe that life consists of more than the things you can see with your eyes, feel with your hands, and prove by arithmetic, you are in poor condition to know the will of God. The man or woman, boy or girl who yearns to know the will of God must believe that there is a God and that he can and will and does communicate his divine wisdom to his children. "He that cometh to God must believe that he is, and that he is a rewarder of them that diligently seek him" (Heb 11:6).

Second, *Jesus used common sense.* The wisdom of Jesus was not far-fetched. It came in the profoundly simple terms of common sense. Jesus talked to common people about things anyone can understand. He knew that a house built on sand cannot stand, that a builder should first count the cost, and that a human life is vastly more valuable than an ox or Sabbath-day observance. The interpretations men of Jesus' day placed on the Scriptures could not withstand the commonsense tests that Jesus applied. Sane judgment is consistent with the will of God. Therefore, Jesus insisted that men allow the will of God to be manifested through the lawful working of their own minds. He said, "He that hath ears, let him hear!" (Matt 11:15). We have ears! Let us use them!

Many of the trivialities that we mistake for great problems fade into nothing when we use common sense. We worry ourselves into early graves over things that good plain horse sense and a healthy sense of humor will solve. Reason teaches us that we cannot get something for nothing. Stable intelligence reveals that God does not reward laziness, stupidity, and littleness with prosperity, brilliant minds, and greatness of character. Common sense teaches that to carry a grudge is to cut off one's nose to spite his face. "Whatsoever a man soweth, that shall he also reap" (Gal 6:7) is so plain that it does not need a theologian to interpret it.

Third, *Jesus devoted himself to honest work*. He worked hard during the thirty silent years as well as during his active ministry. He did not sit for thirty years and dream about the time when he would be the master teacher and physician of Israel. He followed the trade of a carpenter. Jesus dignified labor and revealed the Father as a worker of the vineyard. He said, "My Father worketh hitherto, and I work" (John 5:17). The monks of Cluny spoke aright in their conviction that "to labor is to pray."

Honest labor, then, is a holy exercise, and the will of God becomes clearest to him who labors. Neither my own conscience nor my knowledge of human nature will allow me to believe that God reveals himself to a lazy man. Jesus chose busy men for his disciples. Through the ages, the world's greatest Christians have been those who worked with devotion and diligence. Fishermen, tax gatherers, tentmakers, sellers of purple, housewives, cobblers, mill hands, farmers, physicians, and scholars have followed Jesus the Master Worker. Therefore, in our search for the will of God, it is, as Thomas Carlyle has said, "the first of all problems for a man to find out what kind of work he is to do." And it is not for us to sit idly and dream about that which lies in the dim future, but to do that which lies clearly at hand. Hard work and plenty of it will solve many pains and complaints of people who have time to think only of themselves, criticize others, and make excuses for their laziness.

Fourth, *Jesus searched for the truth*. He sought for the truth anywhere it could be found and promptly submitted himself to it. Jesus said that he came to bear witness of the truth. He clearly taught that the word of God is truth and that the word had been made flesh in him. How, then, can we know the truth? First, by daring to ask what Christ himself would think or do in the specific circumstances in which we find ourselves. But to answer such a question honestly, we must develop a personal knowledge of Christ himself. The person who restricts himself to hearsay about the Christ will never know the truth that makes him free. The opinions of men do not make us free. Too often they enslave us with prejudice. John Locke exclaimed, "I think we may as well hope to see with other men's eyes as to know with other men's understandings."

But even the will to learn the truth for ourselves is not enough. We are doomed to failure if we hope to learn more of the truth without first fashioning our lives after the truth we already know. Someone has said, "It is not the Scriptures I don't understand that bother me. It is the ones that are so clear I can't misunderstand them." Only the person who is reverently dedicated to the doing of the truth ever really knows that truth. Jesus taught that before a man can actually know the truth, he must submit himself in advance to its demands. He closely related the knowing and the doing of the will of God. He said, "If ye abide in my word . . . ye shall know the truth, and the truth shall make you free" (John 8:32). "If any man willeth to do the will of God, He shall know . . ." (John 7:17). John later said, "He that doeth righteousness is righteous" (1 John 3:7). Then if a man is to know the truth, he must, as Immanuel Kant says, desire to let every action be such as could be accepted as a universal standard for all men. Paul approached the good and perfect will of God when he said, "The things that you have seen and heard in me, do . . ." (Phil 4:9).

Fifth, *Jesus loved people because they were people.* He did not love them because they were Jews, because they loved him, or because they had done him a favor. He did not minister to them because he felt it merely his duty to do so. He loved them and ministered to them because they were people. I hardly think the Good Samaritan bound the wounds of the stricken man in order that he himself might inherit eternal life. I doubt that his right hand knew what his left hand was doing. The Samaritan merely saw a man and helped him. It was the natural desire of his heart. When we have such a natural urge to help people, it is God who works in us both to will and to do his own good pleasure. A practical goodwill for all men is the natural overflow of the will of God in our lives. The man who says he knows the will of God and harbors in his heart a grievance against his brother, or has failed to attempt to reconcile himself to a brother who has a grievance against him, is a blasphemer against the name of God. "If a man says he loves God and hates his brother . . . how can he love God whom he has not seen when he does not love his brother whom he has seen?" (1 John 4:20). A great many of us would learn by experience what is the good and perfect will of God if we would act upon this within the week. If we love people spontaneously, compassionately, and intelligently, as Jesus loved them, we have attained unto a great portion of the will of God.

Finally, *Jesus never compromised his faith in the truth and righteousness of God.* Jesus lived intelligently, worked honestly, sought the truth fearlessly, and loved all people regardless of race, creed, and possession. But he lived in a world of ignorance, slothfulness, falsehood, and hatred. That world crucified him. As he prayed in Gethsemane the night of his arrest, his noblest passion was that the will of God might be done in his life. He had such a complete faith in God that nothing could make him quake with cowardice. He could have condemned the bloodthirsty mob for their lack of common sense, but he prayed, "Father, forgive them, for they know not what they do" (Luke 23:34). He could have denied that he was the Son of God, that he had a work to do on earth, but he told Pilate, "To this end have I been born, and for this cause came I into the world" (John 18:37). He could have betrayed the truth that he had proclaimed, but he said that he had come to bear witness of the truth. He could have forsaken the countless generations he had come to save, but he refused to compromise. So they crucified him. Jesus manifested the perfect will of God through his perfect wisdom or common sense, through his absolute devotion to his life's purpose, through his perfect understanding of the truth, and through his complete faith in God. Jesus is the will of God made plain to all people. "Therefore we ought to give the more earnest heed . . . how shall we escape if we neglect so great a salvation?" (Heb 2:3).

14

Guiding Lights for the Caring Pastor

2 Corinthians 4:1-6

Preached at the Alumni Chapel, Southern Baptist Theological Seminary, Louisville, Kentucky, April 3, 1984

John had been arrested. Jesus withdrew to Galilee. He was not to be seen at his hometown of Nazareth. Rather, he settled in Capernaum. Matthew interprets this as his being in "Galilee of the Gentiles." Today the Gentiles are the secular world, both within and without the churches. They are alienated from the life of the church, although the original inspiration of their lives may have been as devout Lutherans, Catholics, Methodists, Church of Christ, and Southern Baptists. They have for complex reasons turned these lights out and choose to grope in the darkness. The words of Matthew describe the situation: "The people that lived in darkness saw a great light; Light dawned on the dwellers in the land of death's dark shadow" (4:16). That Light was Jesus of Nazareth. The Fourth Gospel says of that Light, "All that came to be was alive with his life, and that life was the light of persons" (John 1:4).

You and I are caring pastors to people groping in all kinds of confusion, in darkness, and in death's dark shadow. To those of you who are veteran pastoral counselors, weather-beaten pastors trying to guide individuals and groups, congregations and denominations, I need not tell you of the darkness out there. Life is not like it was in seminary, a matter of courses and A's or C's. Life becomes a matter of life or death; you do live in the land of death's dark shadow. Against the backdrop of this darkness, however, caring Christian pastors have access to many guiding lights for our work. We have this promise and gift in our communion with Jesus Christ. This is made clear to us in the text for this morning:

> Therefore, having this ministry by the mercy of God, we do not lose heart. We have renounced disgraceful, underhanded ways; we refuse to practice cunning or to tamper with God's word, but by the open statement of the truth we would commend ourselves to every man's conscience in the sight of God. And even if our gospel is veiled, it is veiled only to those who are perishing. In their case the god of this world has blinded the minds of the unbelievers, to keep them from seeing the light of the gospel of the glory of God. For what we preach is not ourselves, but Jesus Christ as Lord, with ourselves as your servants for Jesus' sake. For it is the God who said, "Let light shine out of darkness," who has shone in our hearts to give the light of the knowledge of the glory of God in the face of Christ.

In my own ministry, I have found this light of the knowledge of Jesus Christ to refract into a spectrum of awe-inspiring colors as I have sought guiding lights for my own ministry. This light is a many-splendored light. I choose three of the lights from the Scripture that have guided me most often. I commend them to you.

The Pastor as a Steward of His or Her Own Suffering and Comfort. In 2 Corinthians 1:3-7, you see the guiding light for ministry as your personal stewardship of your suffering and the comfort you have received from God:

> Blessed be the God and Father of our Lord Jesus Christ, the Father of mercies and God of all comfort, who comforts us in all our affliction, so that we may be able to comfort those who are in any affliction, with the comfort with which we ourselves are comforted by God. For as we share abundantly in Christ's sufferings, so through Christ we share abundantly in comfort too. If we are afflicted, it is for your comfort and salvation; and if we are comforted, it is for your comfort, which you experience when you patiently endure the same sufferings that we suffer. Our hope for you is unshaken; for we know that as you share in our sufferings, you will also share in our comfort.

Henri Nouwen has given this guiding light of the caring pastor the unforgettable name of the "wounded healer." By Christ's stripes are we healed and by our own stripes we heal others. The generator of wisdom and understanding of others is God's inner revelation to us of the way through our own suffering. God comforts us in all our afflictions. This comfort then becomes the tool and equipment for comforting others. As physicians of the spirits of people, this means that we judge the worth of our therapy by our willingness to take our own medicine. There is a reverse interpretation of the passage. When confronted by the threat of disability, the threat of divorce, the threat of death, are we committed under God to let some of our more courageous counselees' experience be an example to us? Can we learn how to live our lives in the light of God's love in Christ the way some—not all—of them have? As my professor of Church History at Duke used to say to his classes, "Ailing healers are you all, but you will do because God intends it so."

The Mutual Dependence upon God for Forgiveness. A second guiding light I have found for being a caring pastor comes from Hebrews 4:14–5:3:

> Since then we have a great high priest who has passed through the heavens, Jesus, the Son of God, let us hold fast our confession. For we have not a high priest who is unable to sympathize with our weaknesses, but one who in every respect has been tempted as we are, yet without sinning. Let us then with confidence draw near to the throne of grace, that we may receive mercy and find grace to help in time of need. For every high priest chosen from among men is appointed to act on behalf of men in relation to God, to offer gifts and sacrifices for sins. He can deal gently with the ignorant and wayward, since he himself is beset with weakness. Because of this he is bound to offer sacrifice for his own sins as well as for those of the people.

We in pastoral care, both from within and without our own ranks, are often accused of being soft on sinners. We are pilloried for not being confrontational, or lethargic, or just plain downright mean to those who sit in the darkness of sin. The sins we are supposed to be this way about are the obvious ones of sexual infidelity, lack of support of the church, and the excesses of alcohol. We are never urged to lay bare such sins as idolatry, the need to control everyone in one's world, or the preference of living in a dream world and refusing to accept reality. But in either case, without the guiding light of this passage from Hebrews, we are blind guides leading the blind, straining at gnats and swallowing camels (Matt 23:24).

We are urged to know ourselves as sinners and to take our stand with offenders as fellow sinners. We bear patiently with the ignorant and erring. We too are beset by weaknesses. We speak to God on behalf of them. We do not first of all speak to them on behalf of God. What a reversal of conventional pastoral wisdom! We confess our own sins for ourselves no less than for our people. We are ambassadors for Christ's forgiveness and representatives of the people before God as one of them. What a guiding light!

Perhaps the clearest guidance for appreciating, counseling, and caring for the broken-hearted and estranged people we meet comes in the suggestion of an East Kentucky farmer-miner. Robert Coles, a Harvard psychiatrist, has recorded the mountaineer's wisdom for ministers:

> That minister should go and pray for us. He should ask God to give us what we deserve. He should ask God to make him a better minister, so that he'll be able to talk with us and, you know, be more a part of us—know us and not always be giving us those lessons on what we should do and how we should live. He should do some things, too—so he can be better and live better, because it's not just us that have to change our thinking, like he keeps on telling us to do. How does he know what I'm thinking? Has he ever asked me? And has he asked himself—asked himself what he's thinking, and if he should go and change anything in his thinking? He says he wants to help us, but he doesn't really want to see the world as we do. Maybe he should do us a favor and hear us for a change, and then go back to his side of the fence and ask himself if the people over there have anything more important to say.

Coles reacted, "Then I felt close to that minister—and right warned."[1]

Our third guiding light is *The Adoration of Christ*. The two guiding lights I have mentioned thus far are (1) *The Pastor as a Steward of His or Her Own Suffering and Comfort*, and (2) *The Mutual Dependence upon God for Forgiveness*. These lights lay demands upon us. They stress us. They put the heat on us. They test us. Under the leadership of these lights we become battle-tested veterans of ministry. The final guiding light, however, renews us, transforms us, and puts heart into us for the task of caring pastors. The complete and unprismed light for the caring pastor is to adore with steadfast perception the transfigured and transfiguring Christ. Paul tells it like it is in 2 Corinthians 3:18: "And we all, with unveiled face, beholding the glory of the Lord, are being changed into his likeness from one degree of glory to another; for this comes from the Lord who is the Spirit." Herein we become less compulsive and more philosophical about techniques of pastoral care. Here the wells of our patience with the general resistances of human nature are refilled. Here the capacity to find hope where our people can see none is increased. The reason is that we are, through meditation, beholding the Christ and being shaped into his likeness. Thus we are constantly received. As Pierre Teilhard de Chardin said, "Only God can say what this new spirit gradually forming within you will be. Give our Lord the benefit of believing that His hand will lead you, and accept the anxiety of feeling yourself in suspense and incomplete."[2] The writer of 1 John put it this way: "It does not appear what we shall be but we know that we shall be like him for we shall see him as he is. Everyone who has this hope purifies himself, as Christ is pure" (3:2). And Oswald McCall wrote,

> As people see the color in the wave so shall people see in you the thing you have loved most. Out of your eyes will look the spirit you have chosen. In your smile and in your frown the years will speak. You will not walk nor stand nor sit, nor will your hand move, but you will confess the one you serve, and upon your forehead will be written his name as by a revealing pen. Cleverness may select skillful words to cast a veil about you, and circumspection may never sleep, yet will you not be hid. No. As year adds to year, that face of yours, which once, like an unwritten page, lay smooth in your baby crib, will take to itself lines, and still more lines, as the parchment of an old historian who jealously sets down all the story. And there, more deep than acids etch the steel, will grow the inscribed narrative of your mental habits, the emotions of your heart, your sense of conscience, your response to duty, what you think of your God and of your fellow men and of yourself. It will all be there. For you become like that which you love, and the name thereof is written on your brow. There is one revelation of you which must be made.[3]

It must be made.

Notes

1. Robert Coles, *Migrants, Sharecroppers, Mountaineers*, vol. 2 of Children of Crisis (Boston: Little, Brown and Co., 1971) 617.

2. Pierre Teilhard de Chardin, *Hearts on Fire*, ed. Michael Hester, SJ (Chicago: Loyola Press, 1993) 102.

3. Oswald McCall, *The Hand of God* (New York: Harper & Brothers, 1939) 100–101.

15

Remembering and Being Leaders

Hebrews 13:1-7

Memory is a sacred gift. We can misuse it into a curse. We can respect and nourish it into a renewing blessing. By the time one reaches the age of fifty-five, he or she has in the memory an incredibly complex computer filled with massive amounts of data. People say of older people that we become forgetful. The truth is that we have more to remember. We have more that needs forgetting, too. To be able to forget some things is as important as remembering others.

Hebrews 13:7 relates memory to the issue of leadership, that of ourselves and that of those who have led us: "Remember your leaders, those who spoke to you the word of God; consider the outcome of their life; and imitate their faith." You and I are urged to exercise our memories by focusing them on those who have led us in the past. What is the outcome of their lives? What characterized their leadership? What can we learn from their mature years that will enable us to be effective leaders in our church and community in our own "second adulthood"? What do their lives suggest to us about the proper shape of things to come for us in our decision-making and character growth in the years ahead?

Such an exercise in memory prompts us to gratitude. There is no such thing as a self-made person. We are a part of all that we have met. We have had leaders in our lives who gave us a chance. We often call it a "break." They inspired us to adventure, to "take a chance." Courage from their encouragement kindled the life of faith in us. I express here my gratitude for my leaders. A devout public schoolteacher ignored my poverty and responded to my eagerness to learn. She recommended me to my first job as a page in the United States Senate, when I was the ripe old age of thirteen. Leslie L. Biffle, an astute politician, nevertheless had the time to teach me as a page how to conduct my life in a disciplined work schedule, in an appreciation for good manners, and in the use of the English language as a spoken language. He insisted that I know the exact meanings of words and that I pronounce them correctly. Gaines S. Dobbins, my graduate school professor and supervisor, became my spiritual parent in the practice of the Christian ministry and the arts of writing and publication. He insisted on excellence in classroom teaching. I was his apprentice as a teacher.

Time would fail me to tell of all such persons who have led me in the past. The exercise of such memory, however, prompts me to gratitude. My memory of my leaders assures me that the ungrateful life is unfit for a human being to live and remain human. You yourself, I hope, are already making a list of the leaders in your life and assessing what their manner of life and the outcomes of their lives were. As we do this together, we have a lifeline of measurement for the quality of leadership in our own lives. What essential characteristics of their lives stand out? What is it about them that we can imitate in shaping the patterns of our leadership in our churches and communities? I would like to suggest four sterling qualities: answerability, teachability, credibility, and vulnerability.

Answerability. The effective leaders I have known have been characterized by a keen sense of answerability. They saw themselves having a derived authority and not one that arose merely from within them as individuals. Harry Truman in his latest years made this point clear. He said that the [resident of the United States can never safely assume that the playing of "Hail to the Chief" or the discharge of the twenty-one-gun salute was for him. To the contrary, that accolade was for the presidency itself, to which the particular man was always accountable.

We as Christians are answerable to God. We have committed ourselves to God in such a way as to reject all lesser loyalties that claim absolute obedience of us. We make our vows to God first of all and not just to one another. The vows we took in marriage were not made primarily to each other, but to God. We feel answerable to God for the way we care for one another. No earthly father presents either a bride or groom in marriage. God has brought them safely thus far. The commitment to care for and love each other transcends a mere human transaction. I saw a man who approached the age of ninety in prayer, asking that he might live long enough to care for his wife. She had turned against him in her severe mental illness due to the collapsing structures of her brain. However, he still perceived her as his sweetheart. In the power of their youth, he had promised God to care for her until death parted them. God permitted him by reason of strength to survive four heart attacks. Meanwhile he saw to it that his wife was properly cared for. He died ten days after she had died.

Furthermore, we are answerable to our personal "great cloud of martyrs," those who spent and were spent for us. There are those whose suffering is made perfect in our faithfulness to the investment they have made in our lives. We would be true, for there are those who have trusted us; we would be pure, for there are those who care. We would look up and laugh and love and lift. Alex Haley, the author of *Roots*, made this vivid for me as I listened to him in a television interview. He told of having taken a boat from the coast of Africa to America. He asked for the privilege of sleeping in the bottommost part of the boat, just as his ancestors did when they were taken into slavery and brought to America on the slave ships. The pressure of this became so great upon him, added to the insecurity as to whether he would ever be able to write the book, that he fell into deep despair. He tells of one evening going to the deck of the boat and being strongly tempted to commit suicide. That would be the easy way out, and he would be relieved of the responsibility of the book. No one would ever know the difference.

Just as he came to this point, however, he felt the presence of the great multitude of other blacks who had gone before him. He sensed the greatness of their suffering. He could rehearse in his mind the words of Kunta Kinte, Chicken George, and all the others. With one voice, they said in chorus that he should not do this cowardly thing. He should withstand the pressure and, having stood all, stand (Eph 6:13). He says that he was renewed by their company, which reaffirmed his own sense of commitment to be a leader to his people in his day and generation. He wrote the book. We have the results in *Roots*, both in the book and the television story. Alex Haley felt answerable to his own "great cloud of martyrs."

More than being answerable to our own "great cloud of martyrs," we are answerable to our destiny under God. We are called to growth and creativity and not to despair. We refuse to be engineered by the social time clocks of those around us, those for whom we work, or those who would like for us to move over and out of the way so their ambitions can be realized. I personally refuse, for example, to permit anyone to tell me when I am old. I will listen to people who tell me that I am hard of hearing. I will go to a physician to have my ears checked. I will gladly respond to the urgings of people to have my eyes checked if I plan to continue to drive a car. I will appreciate the guidance of those who know how I should take care of my weight, my cardiovascular system, my diet, etc. Yet I know people of all ages who have these needs. These needs should not and will not be "used" on me to disparage my contribution to life by attributing them to age and age alone. I am answerable to my own destiny and cannot leave the decision of aging to anything or anyone except my own sense of destiny under God.

Teachability. In the second place, the leaders I have known have been characterized by an open sense of teachability. They have a lively curiosity about the people and things around them. Jesus spoke of unteachableness as a hardness of heart. This is the sclerosis that we should worry most about if we are truly awake to life: unteachableness. The refreshing and zestful leader is one who works hard at maintaining the capacity of actively listening to other persons, eagerly inquiring into their well-being, and sustaining the ability of accurate empathy for others. My teacher and leader, Gaines S. Dobbins, has recently, at the age of ninety-one, published a book titled *Zest for Living* which bears his witness:

> It was written of Moses that he was 120 years old when he died, and his eye was not dim nor his natural force abated (Deut. 34.7). May I modestly declare that . . . while my eyes have grown dim and my youthful strength is diminished, my zest for learning and teaching has suffered little loss—and I await my transition to a realm where, unfettered by mortality, I shall go on learning and, if permitted, teaching, through an endless eternity![1]

Teachability is the capacity to learn something from most of the people one meets. This is particularly true when we ask if we are teachable enough to learn something from our own sons and daughters. An adult relationship must take the place of our "parenting" of them. In fact, at many points we reverse roles and are parented by our own sons and daughters, particularly when the going gets the roughest. I like the spirit of the mother of a black nurse with whom I work in the Emergency Psychiatry Unit of the University of Louisville School of Medicine's Department of Psychiatry and Behavioral Sciences. She told me that her mother began having children at the age of thirteen. She never got much if any chance to go to school. Yet she saw to it that all of her children got through high school. As each child would return from school, she asked that child to teach her what he or she had learned so that she could learn, too. Mrs. Owens, my nurse colleague, says of her mother, "My mother was a genuinely humble person, a person with a child-like spirit—who could learn from her own children." That is a fresh understanding of humility: openness to learn from others and the world around us. We can say with Walt Whitman,

> Why should I wish to see God better than this day?
> I see something of God each hour of the twenty four, and each moment then,
> In the faces of men and women I see God, and in my own face in the glass,
> I find letters from God dropt in the street, and every one is sign'd by God's name,
> And I leave them where they are, for I know that wheresoe'er I go,
> Others will punctually come for ever and ever.[2]

Credibility. A third characteristic of our leaders that we would do well to imitate is their credibility. Ours is the era of the "credibility gap." Our nature has come through over a decade of trust deprivation. We have lost too much confidence in too many of our leaders in war and peace, church and state, poverty and wealth. We simply have trouble forming attachments to people who do anything more than entertain us. If they have anything to do with the conduct of our lives and the management of our corporate institutions, we lapse into cynicism. When anything goes wrong with a leader or a member of his or her family, then we are prone to say, "It's just as I thought it would be. What else can you expect when people get power and have their hand on the money bags?" As we pass the age of fifty-five, the cumulative disillusionment of such experiences can easily sour us into dyspeptic meanness, disgust, and despair. What alternative do we have? We can search our memories for one or more positive examples of leaders who have sworn to their own hurt and changed not, whose integrity was their prize possession, and who were remarkably believable.

Such credibility has a baseline for concretely measuring the extent to which we are doing the things that create credibility in those who are related to us. One such baseline is the capacity of a leader to share in the responsibility that he or she lays on others. There is such a thing as not being able to delegate responsibility as a leader. There is the opposite extreme, also, of not wanting to accept any of the responsibility but to delegate it all to those who are our underlings. In doing either, we lose credibility. Jesus spoke of the latter kind of leadership in the Pharisees when he said that they bound heavy burdens on others and did not lift one finger to help bear them.

The credible leader, to the contrary, is the person who himself or herself does some of what he or she asks others to do. The pastor who sees himself as the preacher who preaches but does not do any visiting of the people because the people are supposed to do that themselves loses credibility and contact. The administrator who lives off the fat of the land while he or she expects those being led to be sacrificial, to live austerely, and to give beyond their means appears to those being led to be what T. S. Eliot calls a "hollow man." The emptiness of that person's leadership echoes with distrust and loss of credibility.

The antithesis of this is the leader who does what he or she asks of those being led before they are expected to do so. I remember General Tucker, the commanding officer of the paratroop units at Fort Campbell in the mid-1950s. I was asked to come to the base for a workshop with the chaplains. Upon arrival I was taken to the General's Headquarters to meet General Tucker. He was not there, his secretary said, but was out on the "jump field." We went to the jump field and asked for the General. They said he was not on the field. He was in a C-130 plane that was circling above the field. The captain escorting me said, "We have a unit of recruits up there who are on their first jump from a plane. The General has a tradition. He jumps with every group of new recruits. He is always the first one to jump." As he was talking, the C-130 lazily came into position over the jump field and the door swung open. One lone figure stood poised at the door and then jumped. His parachute opened and he came slowly down to the field. He landed on his feet and gathered up his parachute. The General's jeep went out for him and brought him back to where we were. I was introduced to him and I said, "General, you have taught me what real leadership is. You do first what you expect of those whom you lead."

Such leadership inspires confidence and nurtures credibility. I find that students learn how to care for others if I care for them. I find that they are much more convinced of the viability of a given approach to patients if I go with them as we visit seriously disturbed individuals. They become better writers when we share the task of writing together. They become credible themselves if I treasure my own credibility in their eyes. The good leader jumps first when there is any jumping to be done.

Vulnerability. A final characteristic of an effective leader is vulnerability. When you lay your own life on the line in your leadership, you open yourself to the threats of the whole universe. You expose your weaknesses as well as your strengths. You let people know you as you are and not necessarily as you would like to appear in their eyes. To do this is to be vulnerable. Being vulnerable means opening yourself to the possibility of being wounded, hurt, or even destroyed.

If you survive being wounded, you have scars from the encounter. The person who is answerable, teachable, and credible builds in the possibility of being hurt by the irresponsible, the unteachable, and those without credibility. The latter part of the Scripture found in Hebrews 13:1-16 describes Jesus as one who suffered outside the gate of Jerusalem in order to consecrate those who were on the inside of the gate and safe. The creative leader does not see the edge of his or her specific community as the end of the earth, as "the jumping off place." However, the satisfied and seemingly secure within the city tend to see the particular city, denomination, institution, company, etc. as a "flat earth society." Anything beyond the safe confines of that particular organization of persons is "the jumping off place"; the person who ventures beyond its gates is vulnerable to rejection by those within. He or she is likely to be ostracized, hurt, wounded, or even killed by those within. Those within the gates of Jerusalem decreed the death of Jesus. Yet he went outside their gate geographically. He went outside their gate racially. He went outside their gate ethically. The lover of sinners, Samaritans, Syrophoenicians, and publicans was crucified by those of the establishment. He made himself vulnerable. He was wounded for our transgressions. The chastisement of our peace was upon him. He always put himself at risk by loving others.

You and I in our leadership bear the scars of wounds received in action as we have sought to lead. We can remember negative experiences of being hurt by those in whom we placed much confidence and with whom we shared much intimate conversation. We know what it is to be betrayed, left holding the bag, and assigned the task of cleaning up the botched jobs of peers and superiors. We have invested with abandon in people and causes that came to nothing. Our great temptation is to avoid being wounded by ceasing to risk being hurt by even more people. We cannot yield to this temptation in any way. We must continue to take risks, to be vulnerable. We must believe, hope, and endure as the perfect love of God perfects our love by casting out fear. We wear the scars of past wounds uninfected. We are not summertime soldiers of Jesus Christ. We are at the Valley Forge of commitment where the risk is greatest. That makes us leaders tempered by suffering.

You and I as leaders will never be the answerable, teachable, credible people that Jesus was. Yet we are invited to go outside the gate with him and bear abuse for him. We are advised that we have no lasting city. We look for a city that is being brought into being by the kind of leader Jesus was. We are likely to sustain wounds and to carry scars in the process. Yet these scars make veterans of us. The challenge of the later years of life is to see what the scars have taught us. These are scars and not festering wounds of self-pity, vindictiveness, or despair. The challenge of leadership in the mature "second adulthood" is to reinvest what the scars have taught us by being effective tutors of those whom we have chosen to encourage and befriend rather than to see as competitors.

Notes

1. Gaines S. Dobbins, *Zest for Living* (Waco TX: Word Books, 1977) 41.

2. Walt Whitman, "Song of Myself," in *Leaves of Grass* (Brooklyn NY: Dover Thrift, The First [1855] Edition) 9ff.

16

Security in Conflict

John 16:31-33

This sermon was preached by Oates following the attack on Pearl Harbor by the Imperial Japanese Navy against the United States naval base at Pearl Harbor in the United States Territory of Hawaii on the morning of December 7, 1941. The attack led to the United States' entry into World War II.

The whole world is a holocaust of war. One may accurately say with Marc Connelly that "Everything that was nailed down has come loose." The stunned Christian is disgusted with childish solutions of international problems. He has seen too many of them made ridiculous by intelligence and a few hours of history. Jesus Christ alone reveals the course men should follow in finding security for their minds and spirits.

The Sphere of Conflict. Gross human brutality has been made a fact to us in the last few days. We need no theory or imagination to help us describe mass murder, treachery, and international banditry. It would be trite to enumerate the sufferings of innocent people at the hands of ruthless stiflers of human happiness.

In view of such brutality, we naturally choose all sorts of escapisms. We feel as did the leading character of Dorothy Canfield's *Seasoned Timber* when he said, "I took one good look at the work to be done in my generation, and turned and walked off." Some will choose bitter cynicism as a means of escape. Others will toss the reins of their passion to the wind and try to escape through the debauchery of moral laxity and carelessness. Thousands will resort to crude emotionalism disguised as patriotism as a means of expressing their inner confusion. Gullible minds will follow after all sorts of religious fads as a means of deadening the reality of the world malady of war.

But Jesus chose the right way. He saw the world as it actually was. He himself heard the rumble of military forces. He heard the clamors of hunger, wails of entreaty, and exclamations of fear from the distorted human lives about him. He was the object of Herod's brutal cleverness, the victim of the treacherous lies of the Pharisees, and the victim of mob insanity and murder. As he faced Gethsemane, the judgment hall, the scourging, and the crucifixion, Jesus told his disciples, "In the world ye have tribulations" (John 16:33a). He looked steadfastly at the world as it actually was and never resorted to a means of escape. And Jesus demands of us that we learn to see the world as it is without cringing.

The Basis for Security. But how can one keep his heart steady and his mind clear amid the flux of a world at war? When truth seems to be opinion, right a matter of convenience, and goodness a means of deception, what can one call unchangeable, permanent, and secure?

Whence came the calm serenity and peace of Jesus as he faced the stark tragedies of the world? In that moral struggle in the wilderness, Jesus had made some life decisions that proved to be the beams and bolts that held his life together in a time of crisis. He chose to place spiritual values above material values, unseen values above seen values, and eternal values above temporary values. He chose to be a spiritual leader rather than a political reformer. He chose to place the approval of God and an enlightened conscience above the approval of men. These ideals became living facts in the person of Jesus. Outward circumstances did not alter them. To the contrary, his ideals altered the circumstances. The moral truth on which he based his life, work, and ministry was eternal and unchangeable. Wordsworth described such moral truth aright when he said,

> Moral truth
> Is no mechanic structure built by rule;
> And which, once built, retains a steadfast shape
> And undisturbed proportions; but a thing
> Subject, you deem, to vital accidents;
> And, like the water lily, lives and thrives,
> Whose root is fixed in stable earth, whose head
> Floats on tossing waves.[1]

Jesus was spiritually awake to the presence of God in his own life and emotionally dedicated to the purposes of God; therefore, he was not afraid in the presence of danger. Jesus was tossed about by the waves of persecution that swept over him, but, being rooted and grounded in a love for God and men, he never lost his inner calmness and moral collectedness.

Jesus did not promise us freedom from the uncertainty of the physical, political, and international crises that we face. He did not pray that we be taken out of the world. He did not will that we become tender plants in a hothouse of divine favor. But Jesus did promise that if our lives are rooted in him, we will have an inner calmness and serenity that will cause us to grow steadily amid hours of despair such as these.

Let us heed what the Eternal has to say to the temporary. Principles transcend circumstances. Faith in God, the sacredness of human life, moral obligations, truth, and goodness outlive dictators. When the last dictator is only a nightmare of memory, men will still have years to know God and his righteousness. Our present peril is that those of us who claim to have discovered such principles will desert them, and those of us who have not discovered them will continue to be ignorant of them. America is at war; this war must be won. We must not forget, however, that the Christian basis of security is cooperation with God in his desire for peace on earth and good will toward men, and in his inherent love of mercy as well as justice. Let us not allow war to become an end within itself. Gruesome as it is, let us use it as an instrument to end war as soon as possible and to bring peace. America is at war, but the Sermon on the Mount has not been repealed.

Victory in Advance. Finally, Jesus assures us of victory in advance if we are committed to the purposes of God. Before he went to the garden, the judgment hall, and the cross, Jesus told his disciples, "I have overcome the world" (John 16:33b). A flash of insight showed Jesus a panoramic view of his whole life. The past, the present, and the future converged as a spark of eternity in the darkness of time. This exclamation of victory sprang from Jesus' conviction that truth is stronger than falsehood, that good is more desirable than evil, that love and sincerity are more effective than hatred and hypocrisy. With the strength of this conviction released within him, Jesus cut his way forward through his hour of agony. They tried to catch him in error, but he outwitted them with the truth. They condemned him to death, but the awful silence of his peace pricked the conscience of Pilate. They railed at him with jeers, but he prayed that the Father would forgive their ignorance. They killed him, but he committed his spirit to the Father and outlived them. The Roman soldiers said, "He is dead!" but the messenger of God said, "He is not here! He is risen."

In 1942, we shall face the collapse of hopes, the cruelty and stupidity of men, the agony of loneliness, the pinch of want, and the crumbling of world civilizations. But God offers us a basis of security and victory in advance through faith in him. This is God's universe; the wrath of men cannot wrest it from him. The goodness of God will ultimately triumph. The veil of the temples of our souls are now rent with despair; darkness envelops our world; but they who commend their lives into the hands of God will pass through the tomblike darkness. Out of the debris and darkness of shattered hopes will come a fresh realization of the presence of God and the dawn of a new world order.

NOTE

1. William Wordsworth, "The Excursion, Book Fifth, The Pastor," in *The Excursion*, ed. Sally Bushell, James Butler et al. (Ithaca: Cornell University Press, 2007).

Despair: A Disease of the Soul

2 Corinthians 4:8

Despair is the dregs of the cup of human existence. Often in the Stygian darkness of days like these, pure despair grips the soul of even the strongest of Christians. Pushed to our last extremity and haunted by fears without and within, we cry out, "My God, my God, why hast thou forsaken me?"

Why do such hours as these always come? What are the causes of despair? Most human afflictions—however spiritual they may be—have their basis in the physiological organism of the individual. Physical weariness—pure fatigue—arising from a blitzkrieg of responsibilities and continued labor without rest lies at the bottom of most of our futility and despair. As Wordsworth has said,

> The world is too much with us; late and soon,
> Getting and spending, we lay waste our Powers.
> We have given our hearts away, a sordid boon! . . .
> For this, for everything, we are out of tune.[1]

Then, too, people today are genuinely lonely. Each one is pitted in a death struggle against the whole world. He feels himself completely alone, misunderstood, and that no man cares for his soul. How many of us have not felt as the Ancient Mariner felt when he cried,

> Alone, alone, all, all alone,
> Alone on a wide, wide sea;
> And never a saint took pity on
> My soul in agony.[2]

Or, as Shelley has said, some of us feel "This Black Despair. The shadow of a starless night was thrown over the world in which I moved alone."[3] Most of us have felt as Elijah felt in his hour of despair when he cried, "I, even I, am the only one left" (1 Kgs 18:22).

Along with physical weariness and abject loneliness comes frustration. Our world that we have built about us—hopes, ideals, plans, friendships, and devotions—collapse to produce the agony of despair. Our hopes for life's fulfillment are thwarted: maybe we did not get the education we would have desired; maybe it was a disappointment in getting a job, an abashed love affair, the loss of a first child and subsequent childlessness, or the death of a friend or loved one. These latter days have brought the Selective Services Act to frustrate us. Any one or any number of these frustrate us.

Then, too, we are frustrated when our ideals crash about us. We believe in man, but the "sorriness" of man has been brutally revealed to us. We have had people lie to us, betray us, plot against us, and break their treaties with us. It is folly to trust anyone—we think. The ideal of the worth of man can collapse very easily. Then, too, we become estranged or separated from God.

Personal sinfulness is the only thing that can estrange us from God. In our despair we cease to be honest with ourselves. We are prone to shift the blame everywhere and accept none upon ourselves. Sin is the refusal to let God have charge of our lives; it is the refusal to think God's thoughts after him. It is the refusal to let God work his purpose out in our lives. Sin is the attempt to figure out our own destiny without the guidance of God. Sin is taking our lives in our own hands. And the person who is divorced from the will of God, the purpose of God, is miserable; he is in despair because he is sinning against his own nature. As Augustine said, "Thou, O God, hast made us for thyself, and our hearts are restless until they are at rest in thee."

Temptation besieges us when we are in despair. The first temptation is to feel sorry for ourselves. We are prone to heap our own compassion upon ourselves. The second temptation is to quit. Chuck it all overboard. What is the use? Peter had seen the world crucify the Lord, the incarnation of all his hopes, ideals, and purposes. His world crashed about him. And his first impulse was, "I am going fishing." And when we see our efforts going to naught, have the feeling that the things we are devoting our time and energy to are really not worth it all, and we see that no one appreciates the labors we have expended, we feel like throwing it all overboard and going fishing. Often I have felt that my own efforts were futile and have been tempted to shut myself within myself and let the devil pipe his own.

Then, too, we have the temptation to forget the whole thing and have a good time. We'll eat, drink, and be merry, forgetting the sick remembrance of the end. We are lured by this present world and are prone to adopt Omar Khayyam's philosophy when he said to his girlfriend,

> Here with a Loaf of Bread beneath the Bough
> A Flask of Wine, a Book of Verse, —and Thou
> Beside me singing in the Wilderness—
> And the Wilderness is Paradise enow.[4]

As Demas labored with Paul, he could see very little results. He chafed at the incessant labors of evangelizing Asia Minor and the world, and finally Paul said, "Demas left me, having loved this present world" (2 Tim 4:10).

So it is with us. Tempted to quit, tempted by the world, having quit and having loved this present world, we then become the critics of the world. The sour grapes of our own defeat set our teeth on edge. We begin to hurl the cynics' ban, to scoff and sneer. All this while, we are projecting our inner defeats upon those who have not yet partaken of the dregs of human existence. And you see such cynics around you every day: people who are without hope themselves and sit like children in the marketplace and point the finger of criticism at those who, despite their shortcomings, still believe firmly in the worth of man, the goodness of God, and the sacredness of human responsibility to work patiently and constructively for what is good and true, for the redemption of mankind. A. J. Cronin, in his novel *The Keys of the Kingdom*, says, "Hell is where there is no hope." We experience the hell of despair when we give up hope and scorn those who do have hope.

How then can we overcome despair in these dark days? We can never free ourselves from the prison of despair until we admit that there are wicked ways within us. Without genuine repentance there is no hope. David drank the last dreg from the cup of human despair, but he never was free from its poisonous effects until he confessed his sin before God. "All we like sheep have gone astray," said Isaiah (53:6). Isaiah himself was in despair "in the year that King Uzziah died," but he did not find relief until he cried out, "Woe is me; for I am a man of unclean lips" (see Isa 6). Then he felt the forgiving grace of God. And Jesus says to every despairing heart, "Come unto me all ye that labor and are heavy laden, and I will give rest unto your souls . . . Stretch forth your hand . . . Thy sins be forgiven thee" (Matt 11:28; 12:13; 9:2).

Then, too, with such repentance and forgiveness can come a sense of renewal of energy and a burning passion to let God work out his purpose in our lives. An old man once said, "When I was young, I prayed, 'God, help me to do my work.' As I grew older I began to pray, 'Lord, help me to do thy work.' Now I pray, 'Lord, do thy work through me.'" The work of God cannot be accomplished in one generation. A thousand years are as a day in the sight of God. When Isaiah experienced forgiveness from God, he answered with "Here am I, send me" (Isa 6:8).

Along with this fresh committal to the will of God comes the realization that one cannot do the work of God alone. He must seek the fellowship of prayer and work from others. He, realizing his own imperfections, works patiently with those who are likewise imperfect. He seeks to help bear their burdens and finds new meanings and overtones of sympathy when he learns to see the world as God sees it, with eyes of forgiveness and mercy.

The last vestige of despair is driven away when we commit our lives into the hands of God by absolute faith. Jesus was committed to the purpose of God when he said, "Not my will but thine be done" (Luke 22:42). That was belief and consecration. But when the actual test came, faith and faith alone enabled him to say, "Father, into thy hands I commit my spirit" (Luke 23:46). Many of us are going to face the challenges of our hopes, the cruelty and stupidity of men, the agony of loneliness, the pain of hunger, the crumbling of civilization. Pure faith, absolute faith alone, can keep our hearts steady and our heads clear.

The universe is in the hands of God, and the wrath of man cannot wrest it from his control. I doubt not that through the ages one increasing purpose runs, that the goodness of God will ultimately make the wrath of men praise him, and that the generations of men are the stepping stones for the eternal progress of God. The veil of the temple of our souls is rent with despair, and darkness envelops our world, but they who have faith to commend their lives into the hands of God and to walk humbly with him shall surely be led through the tomblike darkness into the dawn, the resurrection of a new life within them and in the world.

Then even the physical weariness shall cease, the roar of cannon shall fade, and men who have been shaken the worst will survive. After a time of calm and sunshine, they will suddenly realize that their Master is on the road of life with them. They will find that he has a new meaning for them. As they walk in his presence, their hearts will be strangely stirred within them. Their minds will be strangely cleared. They will be humiliated by their previous lack of faith and they will be truer to him in his task of world reconstruction.

Notes

1. William Wordsworth, "The World Is Too Much with Us," in *English Romantic Poets*, ed. James Stephens, Edwin L. Beck, and Royall H. Snow (New York: American Book Co, 1935) 70.

2. Samuel Taylor Coleridge, "The Rime of the Ancient Mariner," in *English Literature: A Period Anthology*, ed. Albert C. Baugh and George Wm. McClelland (New York: Appleton-Century-Crofts, Inc., 1954) 824.

3. Percy Bysshe Shelley, "The Revolt of Islam, Dedication: To Mary," Stanza VI, in *English Romantic Poets*, ed. James Stephens, Edwin L. Beck, and Royall H. Snow (New York: American Book Co, 1935) 420.

4. Omar Khayyam, *The Rubaiyat*, trans. Edward FitzGerald. See www.goodreads.com/quotes/475599-here-with-a-loaf-of.

18

THE WRATH OF GOD AND THE DESTINY OF MAN

1 Thessalonians 5:1-11

The principal of the theological college of Bristol University took me on a long walk one evening in his city of Bristol, England. We saw the heavy scars of the bombing raids of World War II. They were now eroded with the passage of eighteen years of weather, weeds, and traffic. He told me that he had been the pastor of a congregation of Baptists in Coventry before World War II. Coventry was one of the most severely battered cities of England during the bombing raids of the Germans. My friend recalled one of the nights when Coventry was most severely bombed. He, no longer being pastor of the church in Coventry, was several miles away from the danger area. But he and his family could hear the fierce noise and knew that the terrible wrath of war was viciously at work. Nevertheless, they retired, hoping that no bombs would come their way before morning. Late in the night a knock came at his door. He answered the door to find one of his former deacons from Coventry. By some means or other he had come all the way from Coventry to see his former pastor. "Come in! What is it that you want or need?" His fellow Christian replied, "I don't want anything, I guess. I just want to tell you that I am alive!" Having thus survived the devastation, death, and wrath about him, he was filled with only one message: "I am alive!"

The Christians to whom the Apostle Paul wrote the First Epistle of Thessalonians lived in such an atmosphere of peril. Being a Christian to them was not a social convenience, a traditional accident, or just another trivial association of people. Being a Christian to them was a matter of life and death. Persecutions were rampant. Christians were not in a "majority that rules." They were a minority group; they were under constant attack. They saw the wrath of man and of God all about them. They had fixed their faith on Jesus Christ who had died for them. Through him they had been delivered up out of the jaws of death. Their urgent witness was, "We are alive in Jesus Christ: Whether we wake or whether we sleep we live in him!" In the midst of this hostile environment and in the presence of the impending end of all things, the Apostle Paul wrote the words of our text: "God has not destined us for wrath, but to obtain salvation through our Lord Jesus Christ, who died for us so that whether we wake or whether we sleep we might live in him" (1 Thess 5:9-10). Then he added the important "therefore" of this promise: "Therefore, let us encourage one another, and build each other up, as indeed you do." The New English Bible translates it, "Therefore, hearten one another, fortify one another—as indeed you do." In this text we see vividly the contrast between the wrath of God and God's destiny for us.

In this text, you and I can clearly see what God's destiny for us is not. God has not destined us for wrath. He has not destined us to live in idolatry and destroy ourselves in the process of it. The word "idolatry" falls on your and my ears with a sense of strangeness. We usually think of idolatry as the worship of statues, relics, the sun, the moon, the stars, or some tangible thing that can be handled with our hands. But our modern idols are not so obvious. We become enslaved to our worship of the next rung on the social ladder. We are prone to worship our work to the exclusion of the rest and renewal in worship that God intended for us when he created us. We become members of various kinds of organizations—many of which are very good—and our affiliation with these organizations often takes first place in our affections. We become involved in social and religious conflicts that we adopt as our main reason for living to the exclusion of the tutelage and guidance of the Holy Spirit. In turning ourselves over to these idols, we give ourselves to the wrath that awaits anyone who directs his allegiance to anything less than the Eternal God above his worship of the living and true God. The Apostle Paul tells us that God has not destined us for this. "He has turned us from idols, to be servants of the true and living God, and to wait expectantly for the appearance of his Son Jesus, whom he raised from the dead, Jesus our deliverer from the wrath to come" (1 Thess 1:9-10). As Paul also tells the Colossians, he would instruct you and me: "Put to death therefore what is earthly in your immortality, impurity, passion, evil desire, and covetousness, which is idolatry. On account of these the wrath of God is coming" (Col 3:5-6).

A part of this, covetousness is evident in the unrelenting hostility men bear toward their neighbors. Paul spoke of the Jews in their treatment of Christians. He spoke of men who are "heedless of God's will and enemies of their fellow man, who hinder the communication of the gospel so that even the Gentiles might have salvation" (1 Thess 2:16). In this he says that such controversies in themselves are so self-defeating that the warring partners fill up the full measure of the wrath of God against them. Such wrath overtakes them for good and all. Even Christians like to think that we can, without punishment, feed our hostility toward our neighbors and hold settled aversions for each other. This is not a temporary irritability or burst of impatience. These are steadfast refusals to reconcile with our brother as did the elder brother in the parable of Jesus. He was angry and would not give in. But as the acid mood of vengeance continues, even Christians can find themselves cut off from their neighbor, from access to themselves and to God by their preoccupation with their settled aversions for each other. The Apostle Paul wrote the book of Thessalonians to some people who had committed themselves to the unhinging effect of meddlesome idleness. They walked in a disorderly fashion. They spent their full time not in productive industry but in discouraging and tearing down one another.

The Apostle Paul says that God has not destined us to this kind of wrath. The Lord Jesus Christ has been raised from the dead. He has turned us to God from our idols to serve a living and true God. He has delivered us from the wrath to come. We are to live as men who have just been rescued from death and are filled with the unwavering expectation of the coming of the Lord Jesus Christ. We cannot, therefore, let ourselves be trapped as the people of God in what a brilliant author of the nineteenth century, Fyodor Dostoevsky, called "the breath of corruption."

In his book, *The Brothers Karamazov*,[1] Dostoevsky tells the story of a group of Russian priests who lived in a monastery. They had a legend that if a man was a truly holy and righteous saint, his body would not smell of corruption, i.e., decay, if he should die. His body itself would be kept intact without odor. If, on the other hand, the body did decay and produced "the breath of corruption," then it would be evident that the man had not been a saint but had really lived an evil life. The leading monk of the monastery, Father Zossima, died. As fate would have it, his body reeked of the breath of corruption. This was a scandal in the monastery. No such thing had ever happened before—they said. But Dostoevsky carefully notes the changes in the attitudes of those who remained alive. The monks fell to arguing among themselves. Some of them said that this proved that no ruling elder could be trusted. Others who were actually jealous of Father Zossima revealed their intense and insatiable hatred of him. Others fell into despair because their idol, Father Zossima, had in death revealed his true humanity. Then Dostoevsky says, "As soon as signs of decomposition had begun to appear, the whole aspect of the monks betrayed their secret motives. Some shook their heads mournfully. Others did not even care to conceal their delight which gleamed unmistakably in their malignant eyes. And no one reproved them for it and no one raised his voice to protest."[2] Such happens today and is the wrath of God extended into our midst. But God has not destined us for this corruptible way of life. This is what God has not destined us for.

When we look at our text more closely, we discover what destiny of man really is: God has not destined us for wrath. He has destined us to obtain salvation through the Lord Jesus Christ so that whether we wake or sleep we might live in him. As Paul also says to the Romans, "Since, therefore, we are now justified by his blood, much more shall we be saved by him from the wrath of God" (Rom 5:8). This is our destiny. Our salvation has been secured, assured, and made real in the death, burial, and resurrection of Jesus Christ. We participate in, we lay hold of, we enjoy, and we draw upon the power of that salvation in Jesus Christ. The power of death cannot separate us from this destiny. Whether we wake or sleep we live in him. As Paul says to the Corinthians, "The love of Christ controls us, because we are convinced that one has died for all; therefore all have died. And he died for all, that those who live might live no longer for themselves but for him who for their sake died and was raised" (2 Cor 5:14-15). Times and seasons of the Second Advent of our Lord Jesus Christ do not preoccupy us. We do not sleep as others do. We keep awake and remain sober. We have been crucified with Christ. Nevertheless, we live. The life we live we live by faith in the Son of God who loved us and gave himself for us. This is our destiny.

In Jesus Christ we discover what our destiny is and learn to redeem every living moment of our time. The same Russian author to whom I referred a few moments ago, Dostoevsky, was condemned to death by firing squad at one point in his life. He had no way out of the death sentence. The Czar had willed that he should die and there was no alternative. He was marched out to a firing squad to be killed. The soldiers loaded their guns. They shouldered them. They cocked their guns to fire. Just at this moment the Czar issued a reprieve. Later Dostoevsky described how he felt as he stood there waiting for death. He said, "What an eternity. I must die. But what if I did not die? Then all eternity would be mine! Oh, then I would change every minute into a century, I would not loose a single one, I would keep track of all my instants, and would not spend any of them lightly." When the reprieve came, it was as if he had actually died and was living a resurrected existence. Therefore, he had no time to waste. He was not just a blind do-gooder who raced about saying happy things and acting as if there was no trouble in the world. To the contrary, his perspective of time had changed by the fact of his having been delivered from death. He could not wait for times and seasons. This was the mood of the Apostle Paul in his writing of the first letter to the Thessalonians. He was appalled at the idleness of busybodies who spent their time fomenting trouble, tearing one another down and disheartening one another. He enjoined the Thessalonians to acknowledge hard work when they saw it among their leaders and guides. For there was no time to waste. Every living moment was an eternity, and every working Christian did his work with the full expectation of the immediate coming of the Lord Jesus Christ. They had no time for idleness. The luxury of purposelessness had to go. The waste of lost motion and the fulfillment of the destiny of God was sin in itself. For every person can expect at any given moment in his personal life to give account of his ministry before the Glorified Lord.

Today there is no time for trifling in the pulpit, the pew, or the school. The idle busybody whose imagination is overweighed with the petty knickknacks of the marketplace, of man's petty self-indulgences, must be challenged. We have not been destined to wrath. But the wrath of God is inevitable when we presume upon the grace of God or exempt ourselves from the responsibility of caring for, encouraging, and edifying each other. We are like Lazarus who had been given a second chance at life. Every moment is a living witness of the power of the living God who died for us in Jesus Christ and has brought us into the realm of the resurrection. When we go anywhere, it is not to get something for ourselves. We go to report the good news that we are alive in God through Jesus Christ. This mission is our destiny.

Finally, the Apostle Paul gives specific guidance to us as to what we are to do in the fulfillment of our destiny. As was customary in his writings, Paul brings his great doctrinal statements to a climax with a "therefore": "Therefore, encourage one another and build one another up." The deliverance of the Christians from wrath and his assurance of salvation are not, in Paul's words, something that he holds in a private soliloquy with God. Note that Paul says, "Encourage one another. Build up one another." The destiny of freedom from wrath and participation in salvation involves us with one another in a community of trust and care. The test of our basic beliefs and doctrines is in our relationships to one another. The purpose of our faith in Jesus Christ and redemption from the wrath to come is that the covenanted community of the people of God may care for, encourage, and build each other up in this faith and declare that faith to those on the outside. That which we have experienced with God in Christ we declare unto them that they may have fellowship with us and that the blood of Jesus Christ will cleanse them of sin, too.

Paul says we are to encourage each other. To encourage means to "hearten," to put heart into, to sustain and nourish each other. Someone says that encouragement is literally "lending ourselves" to our neighbor. Barnabas was a "son of encouragement." Being filled with the Holy Spirit himself, he inspirited and animated others. He raised their confidence in each other and brought hope to them when they were in despair. This he did for the Apostle Paul. This he did for John Mark. We have records of this "ministry of encouragement," and I am sure that the unwritten events would cause us to marvel even more at the way in which Barnabas "encouraged" his fellow Christians and emboldened, invited, and inspired them to expect great things of God and attempt great things for God.

As you look about you in your church, do you find people who live in quiet despair? Who do you know who is disheartened? Have they met anyone in the church who is a minister of encouragement? Is anyone called to put heart into people and to undergird them in the works of light that they do while it is day? If not, you can be that person to them. In the brevity of our existence, life is too short for making another person's task either more difficult for him or impossible for him. We are called to undergird, sustain, support, and put heart into each other. This is our destiny as children of light.

And again we are called to build each other up. In another portion of the Scripture the Apostle Paul put it this way: "And now, my friends, all that is true, all that is noble, all that is just and pure, all that is loveable and gracious, whatever is excellent and admirable fill all your thoughts with these things" (Phil 4:8, New English Bible). The living hope of the return of the Lord Jesus Christ cannot be separated from these disciplines of edifying and building up the fellowship of believers. The Apostle Paul says, "Live at peace among yourselves, admonish the careless, encourage the fainthearted, support the weak and be patient with them all. See to it that no one pays back wrong for wrong but always aim at doing the best you can for each other and for all men. Be always joyful; pray continually; give thanks whatever happens; for this is what God in Christ wills for you"

(1 Thess 5:14-18, New English Bible). God has not destined us to wrath but that we should obtain, enjoy, participate in, and make real in our relationships to each other the salvation that only the Lord Jesus Christ has brought us.

If we find our brother overtaken in a fault, we who are spiritual have been called of God to restore such a one in a spirit of gentleness, looking to ourselves lest we also be tempted. There is a law of the spirit which says that the more we want to tear a brother down for his misdemeanor, the more likely it is that we ourselves are secretly guilty of the same sin for which he is exposed. To the contrary, the person who has been redeemed from the destruction of the wrath to come is least willing to tear down and destroy his neighbor or to profit by his downfall. He seeks to edify, to build up, to restore, and to follow the pattern of confrontation, instruction, and resurrection of new life in Jesus Christ. He does not do this because he is a great statesman, a clever manipulator of men's lives, or even because he is a good man. He does this because he has faced the total destruction of his own life in death and been redeemed from it by Jesus Christ. He lives no longer for his own sake but for the sake of him who died for him. He builds up his brother not because he is a special friend of his, not because he particularly likes or dislikes him, but because this person is a person for whom Christ died and from this comes his value as a person apart from this or that wrong thing he may have done. Thus our relationships to each other have an objective, unchanging, and ultimate foundation in Jesus Christ and not merely in the shifting moods we feel toward each other from day to day. We are bound together in the new covenant of the blood of Jesus Christ and not merely by our personal likes and dislikes.

Such a concern for each other within the Christian fellowship spills over into the witness of the good news of Jesus Christ to those who are not Christians. I shall never forget an occasion in which I, as a pastor of a rural church, sought to win a young man and his wife to Christ with no success. Several months later this young man and one of his friends were stealing some wild honey from the farm of one of the deacons of our church. The deacon came upon him in the very act. The young man and his accomplice ran when they saw the deacon coming. They were new in the community and our deacon knew the shorter way to their house. When they arrived there, he was sitting on the front porch. They were desperately frightened that he would "call the law," as is the first thought of many people when it should be the last thought of a Christian. But in their amazement the deacon was not angry with them. He said, "You were trying to steal honey from a place where it is really no good. I have some better honey than that and I want you to go with me and I will show you where it is and you can have all you want." They became friends. The deacon encouraged them and built them up. About ten months later, the young man and his wife, whom I had failed to win to Christ, of their own accord came upon a profession of faith one Sunday morning. Encourage one another. Build one another up. Both you and your non-Christian neighbor will bring forth fruit in the kingdom of God.

Notes

1. Fyodor Dostoevsky, *The Brothers Karamazov*, trans. Constance Garnet (New York: International Collectors Library) 305ff.

2. Ibid., 309.

Part II: Prayers

Introduction

Throughout his writings, Wayne Oates reminds ministers and laity of the importance of prayer in their personal lives and in their ministry to others. In his book, *Nurturing Silence in a Noisy Heart*, he offers his readers some directions on how one might find serenity and silence in the fast-paced and noisy world in which we live. He directs us to respond to the call of serenity and silence where we can hear others, our own deepest needs, and most of all the presence of God.[1] In referring to the Lord's Prayer, he asserts that the petitions in this prayer are fervent appeals to God to provide for us with the assurance that God is intimately involved in the process of life. He notes, however, that the Lord's Prayer offers no resort to magic and calls on our full responsibility for the necessary disciplines to respond to God and not transfer or project responsibility to others. He also observes that this prayer is free of religious ideologies and includes all people of any faith perspective who believe in God.[2]

In the counseling process, Oates reminds ministers and other counselors that "prayer is one of the inexhaustible sources upon which the pastor draws in his counseling ministry."[3] The counselor draws upon prayer for personal strength as he or she helps bear the burdens of others as well as giving support to those who are being counseled. Oates believes that the Bible is an invaluable aid to prayer, predominantly because it is a book of prayer itself. He draws upon some of the great prayers from the Bible and offers a number of paraphrases that can be used in times of counseling like for a "Discouraged Married Couple, "A Perplexed Doubter," "In the Midst of Suffering," "A Prayer of Thanksgiving," and others.[4] Drawing upon Augustine's view that "our heart is restless until it rests in God," Oates speaks of the "prayer of rest." Prayer as "rest" summons us to waiting in the presence of God and seeking to glorify God and enjoy God forever. Resting in God's presence allows us to experience forgiveness that sets us free. This forgiveness releases and pardons our personal sins and also enables us to let go of our sins toward those who have wronged us. Having experienced the forgiveness of God, we respond with thanksgiving and graciousness.[5]

Before a pastor can assist another person's spiritual quest, he or she, Oates affirms, has to be a spiritual person of prayer. "The pastor's private worship life is the beginning of our own response to 'serious call to a devout and holy life,'" he wrote.[6] This is essential, he believed, because he interpreted the interpersonal ministry of caring for people as a form of prayer itself. A strong personal prayer life for the counselor will enable her to keep her confidence in people strong, prevent her from losing patience with them, and give her an inner calmness when dealing with severe troubles and unhappiness. Oates believed that a pastor or counselor "brings the assurance of God through prayer." Conversation with God should be handled as "prescriptively as any powerful medicine." To do this effectively, Oates cautioned the counselor to use prayer appropriately and not in an atmosphere of frivolity or gossip, and to avoid trite or worn-out phrases. Sometimes rather than a formal prayer, because of the lack of privacy or quiet, one might say something like, "Remember, I will be praying for you as you face your challenges tomorrow." Prayer should not be used, he believed, as a means of simply ending a visit.[7]

Oates considered prayer so important that he urged pastors and counselors to bathe all aspects of their ministry in an atmosphere of constant prayer. Three years before his death in 1999, he compiled a collection of biblical prayers drawn from the Old and New Testament and titled *Grace Enough: Timeless Words for Trying Times*. The book was published in a convenient pocket size for use in the common occurrences and crises of life.[8] In his spoken prayers, Oates avoided clichés and formal or commonplace phrases, nevertheless keeping his prayers simple, focused, and personal. The prayers included here are selected from prayers Oates offered in churches, seminary classrooms, the seminary chapel, and other places. If the occasion or purpose of the prayer is known, it is noted above the prayer. He often used the language of the King James Version of the Bible in his prayers, and I left them as written. I also did not change them to use inclusive language, even though I believe he would use it today. The beauty, simplicity, and religious depth of these prayers are examples of genuine spiritual devotion.

Selected Prayers

Crises as "End Situations"[9]

O Lord God, who in Jesus Christ dwelt with us in human form, you know what both time and eternity are. You have made everything beautiful in its time and you have set eternity in our hearts. We are acutely aware of the ends you have set to hours, days, weeks, months, years, and lives. We feel the shortness of time in the pressed crises of our own lives. Teach us how to feel our ways into the time-bends of the crises of those to whom we minister. Grant unto us the wisdom to sense when the different times of people's lives come to an end and call for death to an old self and birth to a new self. Grant unto us the foresight to be able in your strong name to interpret to them the shape of things to come. But above all, cleanse us of any sense of despair ourselves in order that we may be harbingers of hope to people who are tempted to give up on themselves, on others, on life, and even on thee. Through Jesus Christ who gives us hope we pray. Amen.

Crises as "Leaps of Faith" vs. "Shrinking Back"

Our God, who rules and reigns even when we are faint-hearted and weak-kneed in the presence of the demands of maturity, we confess to you that it plainly seems safer to take no risk and to keep the gifts you have given us just as they are for ourselves and ourselves alone. If you will not disturb us with the business of growing, we will stay just as we are, if you don't mind. With thoughts like these, see how easily we delude ourselves. What we are not yet confessing is that our fears cause us to shrink back and lose our very integrity of being. Your truth goes marching on while we lay back.

Let your perfect love cast out this fear. Fill us with courage to put away childish things, to head straight into and through the crises of our own lives. Then, even as you have strengthened us to take the leap of faith in thee, help us to use this power to strengthen brothers and sisters who themselves are being tempted to shrink back. In the name of him who for the joy that was set before him endured the cross we pray. Amen.

Crises as Emergencies or Threats to Survival

Loving God, you have made yourself known to us in the strong being of Jesus Christ our Lord. Your Holy Spirit has brought to our remembrance his teaching that life is fragile, time is always shorter than we think, and death separates itself from us by a thin partition that can be sundered in a split moment of emergency. Therefore, teach us today how to be alert, to be wakeful, and at the same time be discerning, wise as serpents and as harmless as doves as we assess, lay hold of, and deal with the emergencies presented to us as undershepherds of Jesus Christ. For it is in his wisdom that we live, and move, and have our being. Amen.

Crisis Accumulation as Stress

O God, you have entrusted into the earthenware of our beings the treasure of the ministry of your word to people in times of stress. When we are hard-pressed to know how to fulfill this ministry, grant unto us the gift of discernment. When we are bewildered, perplexed, and overwhelmed, rouse within us the wits and intelligence with which you have endowed us. When we are beset by those who would do us in, grant that what they mean to us for evil we may see what is in it that you mean to us for good. When we get knocked down, give us renewed life to get up in renewed strength to serve you. When we lose the capacity to laugh, help us to see the ridiculous irony of human foibles—including our own—and to laugh once again. In the name of him who gives us a hope in the power of his resurrection that never disappoints us we pray. Amen.

O God, you have entered our realm of temptation, stress, and suffering fully in Jesus Christ. We are not homeless, though we may feel very far from home. You and your Son have come in the presence of your Holy Spirit and made your home with us. We become aware of our at-homeness with you when we sense the depths of our love for you.

Today as we endure our own stresses, enable us to draw from your at-homeness with us the power to discern, appreciate, and respond with accurate empathy to those we meet today who are themselves under greater stress than we are. Through the strong name of Jesus Christ our Lord we pray. Amen.

O God, if anyone is going to lead us into times of temptation and testing, we want it to be you and no one else, especially the devil. We know that you know the limit of stress we can bear. You love us and will not overstep the limits you set for us when you created us. Yet within those boundaries, grant that training in the way of Christ that will make us able to outwit, bear, and use the stresses that are our daily lot.

Once you have strengthened us in times of testing, help us to turn and strengthen our comrades and become teachers to them. We come to you today with all of the stresses each of us has, and we are bold to do so as we seek timely help in the name of him who was tested in every way just as we are—Jesus, your Son. Amen.

Stress Management and Pastoral Care

O God, our help in ages past, our hope for years to come, be thou our shelter from the blast, and our eternal home. O God, the central peace and the source of all ministry in the universe, we come to you with gratitude for the complete interpretation of life and its stresses that you have given us in Jesus Christ our Lord. We are awed that you have put us to the task of being interpreters of our people's stresses to you in petitions and prayers and to them in discernment and the power of carefully chosen words. Help us to feel the weight that speaking of and for you provides us. Help us to be slow to speak, ready to watch and listen, and caring in our response to those to whom we minister. Help us to heal sometimes, to remedy often, and to care always in your holy name. Amen.

O Lord our God, how great you are! We rejoice in the mission of Jesus Christ in our lives that we too shall not only care for those who are safely in the fold, but that we shall minister to the captives, the blind, the oppressed, the outcasts, the untouchables, the unlovely and unlovable. Sometimes we are shaken by the terror of the task. So let us always hasten to you for courage and wisdom, yes, but above all for companionship in the calling to which you have called us. Through Jesus we pray, whom we love, whom we serve, and like whom we want you to make us. Amen.

A Pastoral Interpretation of Stress and Stress Management

O God, we thank you for the prayer of Jesus for those who have received your gifts, your teachings, and your certainty from him. We dare to lay hold of these for our own certainty in doing the ministry to which you have called us. As we begin to converse together, let your presence cause our hearts to come to new life and hope as we seek to learn from each other in the community. Be our vision, our commander, and our buffer against confusion. May we listen to each other's words, understand each other's meanings, and find wisdom together that only you can create. Through Jesus Christ our Lord we pray. Amen.

O God, whose all-inclusive love and wisdom fills the whole earth with your mystery, your revelation, and your glory, so help us to discipline our minds in your ways of perceiving the world that nothing will be secular to us. Grant unto us the patience to learn the languages of your word and the languages of those who serve you without knowing it to heal the hurts, to mend the relationships, and to fulfill your creation in those whom we serve. Through Jesus Christ our Lord we pray. Amen.

Pastoral Initiative and Crisis Intervention

We praise you, O God, for taking the divine initiative toward us in our darkness, our sin, and our stupidity. You came to us in Jesus Christ when we would have been too afraid, too proud, and too self-sufficient to come to you. His love overcame every barrier and continues to plumb the depths of every human concern of ours. We bless you and are blessed by you in your visitation of us in the marketplaces of our lives to lure us away from each idol that would possess us and to free us from its demonic power. Forbid that we should keep the good news of your liberation of us a secret. Help us to be good stewards of the initiative you have given us in our entry into the crucial human situations of our neighbors. Through him who stands at the door of our hearts and knocks we pray. Amen.

The Life Support System and Crisis Management

O Lord our God, when we consider the faces of those to whom you have ordained us to minister, we tremble at the thought of having to do this singlehandedly, alone. This is too much for us. Forbid that we get so wrapped up in one person's needs that we ignore the Body of Christ of which both they and we are a part. Save us from the fate of being cancerous tissue in the tissue of the Body of Christ, acting apart from the divinely ordered systems of Christ's own Body here on earth.

Prompt in us gratitude and humility for the fellowship of people of shared commitment to you and the care of your hurting ones. Fill us with the zest of comradeship in caring for others. As we are bonded to persons of skill, clean hands, and pure hearts, let us all celebrate your Lordship. Right here and now, grant unto us the sense of kinship so that the very system of our relationships will be a healing grace to each other and, together, to people we share concerns about in ministry. Through Jesus Christ our Lord. Amen.

Our God, in whom we live and move and have our being, search us and know our hearts, try us and know our thoughts, and see if there is any wicked way in us, and lead us in the way that is everlasting. Through the strong name of Jesus Christ we pray. Amen.

The Crises of Grief and Separation

Our God, who art the God of the living and not the dead, as we come to consider the power of grief to overwhelm us and those to whom we minister, forbid that we lose sight of the power of the resurrection of our Lord. Grant unto us fresh confidence that nothing—neither life nor death, nor things present nor things to come—can separate us from your love in Jesus Christ. As you strengthen us, help us to strengthen one another and all who seek our aid in times of grief. Through Jesus Christ we pray. Amen.

Our Lord and our God, we find the ministry to the grief-stricken too heavy for us to bear alone. When we open our mouths to comfort people, words either won't come to us or turn out to be limp excuses for comfort. Let your Spirit come to our aid in these moments and in our weakness. We rely on Your Spirit to intercede for us and those to whom we minister in our wordlessness. Plumb the depths of nonverbal expressions of comfort and make them available to us and our fellow strugglers in grief. Through him who was and is thoroughly acquainted with grief, Jesus Christ, we pray. Amen.

Our Lord and our God, we bless you for the vision and the hope of a new heaven and a new earth, for a sphere of being in which death, mourning, crying, and pain shall be no more. We are renewed by this faith and hope, and may it root us and ground us in courage as we minister to the dying and bereaved. We thank you for Jesus Christ, the resurrection and the life, in whom death itself is dead. Amen.

The Crises Surrounding Birth

O God, the Giver of life and the Mystery of life's dilemmas, we marvel at the wonder and intricacy of the human conception and birth process. Forgive us for being and thinking so casually and shallowly about it that we assume we know all about it. We confess our ignorance and irreverence to you. Teach us the patience and discipline of close attention and a search for facts about human birthing. Thus we shall be wiser and more compassionate parents. Thus we will be more considerate and faithful pastors to people who invite us into their lives at the time of the birth of a child. In the name of him who came to us as a tiny baby, Jesus our Lord. Amen.

O Lord, our God, we are fearfully and wonderfully made. You are at work in the minds of parents and in the process of conception, gestation, and birth of little babies. We glorify you for involving us as parents in your creation and pray in this hour, as did Manoah (see Judg 13–14), to give us your guidance in what manner we should take in the responsibility of our children whom we are entrusted by you as their parents. Through Jesus Christ, your only begotten Son, we pray. Amen.

O Lord, our minds stagger and our hearts sink within us when we realize even a few of the things that can go wrong in the conception and birth of children. We know that your own creation catches most of these mistakes and corrects them. We thank you for revealing to us remedies and technologies in which we can participate with you in preventing others. Reveal to us those secrets yet unknown whereby every child possible will be born healthy and well formed.

    Meanwhile, curb our anger at the mystery behind these defects and put up with our impatience with you and ourselves. Above all, help us to be faithful companions to parents and all of your little ones regardless of their plight. Through Jesus our Lord we pray. Amen.

The Crises of Physical Illness and Trauma

O God, we bless you for the gift of the Holy Spirit. In the Spirit, you and your Son come and make your home with us. You have not left us as orphans. You dwell in our mortal bodies, and our bodies are temples of the Holy Spirit. We are not our own. We cannot do with our bodies as we please and still please you. Teach us to discipline our bodily habits to make them clean, healthy, productive instruments of your peace. Help us to lay aside every habit that contaminates or misuses and abuses our bodies. We present our bodies to you as living sacrifices to demonstrate what you would have us demonstrate to those to whom we minister. Amen.

O Lord our God, we have trouble believing that we are mortal, that we die natural deaths, that you have set the bounds of our natural lives. Thus we are frightened when we are called upon to minister to the dying. We have trouble accepting the limits of our own abilities when we are in excellent health. Therefore, we are terrified when we are asked to be faithful companions in ministry to badly damaged and handicapped persons. O God, free us from being paralyzed by the fear of death and thus unable us to function as your ministers, and free us of our terror in the face of human handicaps. We know that you do not put us to tests beyond what we can bear. Through the power of your Spirit, help us to stand and, having stood, to stand all in the name of Jesus Christ our Lord. Amen.

The Crisis of Marital Conflict

Our God and our Home, we yearn for both the tenderness and courage of Jesus Christ our Lord. We hunger for his wisdom as of the serpents and his harmlessness as of the doves. In this earthly and earthy relationship of husband and wife, we need these graces and gifts. We yield ourselves up to you in personal discipline that you may bring these to pass as we are crucified with Christ day by day. We die to hardness of heart and are raised to be tenderhearted, forgiving one another. We die to blindness and to refusal to put ourselves in each other's place. We are raised to dwell with husband or wife with understanding and considerateness. Thus in living as joint heirs in the grace of life, we find all hindrances to face-to-face prayer with you removed. Thank you, Lord, in the name of Jesus. Amen.

Our Loving God, we pray for all families who are at odds with each other, locked in impasses of misunderstanding and hurting each other with words and deeds. We ask for a new centering of their affections on you and a fresh appreciation of each other's human frailties. Divest husbands and wives of all greediness of desire to be satisfied and pleased at all times. Reduce their desires for material things to that which is needed that they may have time, attention, care, and tenderness for each other. Bring rest to them in their fatigue, unselfish guidance to them in their decisions, and a renewed commitment to their marriage. May they be equally yoked together in this commitment. Thus bring certainty into their lives and those of their children. And may they dwell in such harmony that they may with one voice glorify the Lord Jesus Christ. Amen.

The Crisis of Divorce

O Lord, our Lord, you have told us as we go forth as your disciples to be wise as serpents and harmless as doves because you are sending us as sheep among wolves. Sharpen our wisdom, therefore, O Lord, as we seek to interpret your word to people who are divorced. At the same time, enable us to be gentle and considerate as we hear their stories and as they frame their questions. Help us to be quick to hear, slow to speak, and always seeking for the words and tones of voice that edify, bring hope, and yet represent reality to our flock. We approach these tasks as fellow sinners with those we seek to guide. Therefore, we confess our sins and especially our hardness of heart to you. Forgive us, we pray, and enable us to walk confidently in your love. Amen.

The Crisis of Depression

Our God and Lord of our lives, we come this morning to consider our ministry to others in that dark night of the spirit we call depression. We look within us through any dark desperation we have or have ever felt for your light in how depression feels, how it makes us think, and what your sources of encouragement, hope, and joy in life are. Heal us of weariness of spirit through your renewing grace. Grant unto us the oil of joy for the spirit of mourning and the mantles of praise for the spirit of heaviness. Through Jesus Christ our Lord. Amen.

Lord, who has been our dwelling place through all generations, grant unto us the gift of discernment of the spirits that come upon us to stifle the joy of your people. Grant unto us the patience and the courage to take action on behalf of those who are depressed. Grant unto us extra measures of hope that we may share it with those who have given up hope. Grant unto us patience that we may stand steadfastly with them in their dark days and not run from them. But above all, grant unto us your presence, for you are the God of both the darkness and the light. In the name of him who is the Light of the World, Jesus Christ our Lord, we pray. Amen.

O God, our Sustainer in Jesus Christ, sometimes our words stick in our mouths when we give thanks for our limitations, our handicaps, and our adversities. We grit our teeth as we say so. Yet say so we do. At the same time, we ask that you will take our weaknesses and make them turn out to your glory, honor, dominion, and power. Use them to increase our understanding of and empathy for people who open their hearts in trust to us as servants of yours. With the comfort with which you comfort us, equip us to be a comfort to them. Through Jesus Christ. Amen.

The Crisis of Suicide

Dear Lord and Sustainer of our lives, forbid that we should put you to the test by taking the matter of our own death into our own hands. Grant unto us both the wisdom and the winsomeness to persuade those who despair of life itself to rely upon you and to hope in you. O love that never fails, give unto them and to us fresh sources of energy and a firm confidence in the hope that never disappoints, Jesus Christ Our Lord. Amen.

Our Lord and our God, when we have done something wrong in our own eyes that cuts us off from all those whose approval we have thought most worthwhile, speak to us with forgiving impulses of your Spirit. Keep us back from presumptuous folly and lead us into full confession of our sins to you, the Lord of Life. Then lift us up by the power of your forgiving love to reconcile us to those we have wronged and to our own best selves. Then, our God and our Redeemer, we will treasure each moment of each day and offer it up as a sacrifice of service to you and your Son, Jesus Christ our Lord. Amen.

The Crisis of Psychotic Breaks with Reality

O God, who helps us to see life, ourselves, each other, and you yourself clearly, grant unto us that spirit of power, of love, and of a sound mind for which we yearn. Reclothe us in our rightful minds day by day. Grant unto us a spirit of discernment that we may bring those whom fear has overcome and suspicion has taken over a calm and steady walk of life. We pray for all those who are beside themselves and distracted by the horrors of the nethermost regions of the human mind. Grant unto them your healing grace and to all of us who care for them your understanding, wisdom, and patience. Through Jesus Christ our Lord. Amen.

Our God, who art always with us in the turbulent sea of suffering into which this course thrusts our timid spirits, we thank you for the vision of the New Jerusalem and the promise of the resurrection. We are renewed with hope when tempted to give up on individuals, families, churches, and our world. We thank you for the hope that your resurrection of Jesus can be a daily event in our despair. We are crucified with Christ daily. Yet we live daily. Yet not we but the resurrected Christ lives in us. Therefore, may the life we live this day be by faith in the Son of God who loved us and gave himself for us. Amen.

The Crises of Educational Mobility and Alienation

O God, who in Jesus Christ did come at this season to your own and your own received you not, we remember this morning all who at this Christmas season dread visiting the hometowns. We think of them as they try to communicate with their family of origin and their home churches over the barriers that may be there without name but with great resistance nevertheless. May we in this hour sense some of the shapes and forms of their loneliness, find fellowship with them, and put into words some of their unspoken anxieties. Be our vision, our counselor, and our leader in your Holy Spirit, through Jesus Christ our Lord we pray. Amen.

Lord, in our efforts to win acceptance from our clan and kin, forbid that we hasten ahead of your clear calling and instructions. Keep us back from poor judgment, rash acts, and fear-ridden behaviors. Discipline us in the wilderness away from our own kind. Give us the patience to wait for the openings of your Spirit to serve with gladness and strength our own kinspersons in your way, your time, your strength, and your wisdom. Through Jesus Christ we pray. Amen.

The Crises of Religious Alienation: Social and Spiritual

Our God, who in Jesus Christ is always at work in reconciliation of those who are estranged and alienated from each other, we thank you that the person who does your will is our mother, father, brother, or sister. We glorify you for the larger family of the people of God that puts our earthly families in their rightful context. Yet comfort us in any distance we feel from them. Be our teacher and enable us to have open hearts, tender hearts, wise hearts, and teachable hearts as we relate to our own flesh and blood.

Reconcile us where we are alienated. Comfort us when loneliness ensues as our reconciliation is rebuffed. In the name of Jesus Christ we pray. Amen.

For a Person Who Is Dying

Oates shared this prayer in a letter from a person who heard him pray it for someone who was dying. He asked for a copy of it so he could use it with others in similar circumstances.

O God, we thank thee for the gift of life thus far we have received so bountifully from thy caring hand. We bless thee for thy presence here now, for we know that thou art always near. We ask your gift of courage and will to life of [name]. We ask that he/she may sense our love and your love upholding him/her. We know that the fullest length of life is always wanting to raise death from life. We know that death is a part of thy creation of all creatures. Yet we thank thee that neither death nor life, things present nor things to come can separate us from thee and thy Son, Jesus Christ. Grant [name] a serenity and inner peace from the knowledge of thy eternal love. In the name of him who died, who was raised from the dead and lives evermore, Jesus Christ our Lord, we pray. Amen.

Prayer of Dedication for Families

Our parently God, in whose image abides both male and female in the oneness of your majesty, we thank thee that every family on earth and in heaven is named after thee. We pray that thou wilt strengthen us as families with the power of your Spirit within the private conversations we have with each other at home, on the telephone, and in our letters to each other. We ask that we may be teachable by thy Spirit as thou dost reveal thyself to us in what our husbands, wives, sons and daughters, brothers and sisters say to us. Save us from hardheadedness and hardheartedness unto a tender and teachable heart toward each other.

Grant us the grace and courage to let each other grow, to be warm but not possessive in our love for each other. Give us the gift of laughter at our own pettiness and the gift of greatness of heart when we are offended by each other.

Save us, we pray, from the tender idolatry of each other that limits our ministry to people in our own families. We thank you for Jesus and his family who permitted him to reach out to all mankind, and especially unto us, as well as to them.

Teach us to have the honesty and curiosity, the love and trustfulness of little children. We dedicate our ambitions for our children to thee. May each father's heart here be turned to his children. May each mother here be revered on this Mother's Day for her participation with you in giving life and love to the rest of us.

Now, may the God who gives perseverance and encouragement grant that we may be of the same mind with one another in Christ so that with one accord we may glorify thee, O God, the God and Father of our Lord Jesus Christ. Amen.

Closing Prayers[10]

God of peace, grant unto me the discipline and spiritual integrity that reconciliation with you and fellow human beings provides as I take up my cross this day and follow the Lord Jesus Christ. Amen.

Lord God, by the grace of your Son, Jesus Christ, and leadership of your Holy Spirit, enable us to live lives of sincere worship that leads us to care for the oppressed, share bread with the hungry, find shelter for the homeless, and break the bonds of wickedness. Amen.

Almighty God, in whom we live and move and have our being, establish us in great habits of gratitude and worship of you. We thank you for all your benefits. Amen.

Various Prayers

A prayer before the sermon "The Wrath of God"
Our Heavenly Father, direct us unerringly to the open places in the hearts of our hearers. Make each of us—speaker and hearer—to increase and abound in love for all men. Establish us together with unblameable hearts before thee, our Father. Prepare all our lives for the coming of the Lord Jesus Christ with all his saints. (Paraphrase of 1 Thess 3:11-13)

Concluding prayer of the sermon "The Wrath of God"
May our God and Father himself and our Lord Jesus Christ bring this message directly to you. May the Lord make your love mount and overflow towards one another and towards all as our love does towards you. May he make your hearts firm, so that you may stand before our God and Father,

holy and faultless when our Lord Jesus Christ comes with all those that are his own. *(Paraphrase of 1 Thess 3:11-13)*

Pastoral prayer, August 4, 1991, St. Matthews Baptist Church, Louisville, Kentucky
Almighty God, Giver of life and Sustainer of our hopes, we lift unto you all of those who are suffering illnesses and bereavements in our congregation, all those who are suffering bereavements that are not so obvious—maybe the loss of a job, maybe the inadequacy of a job to make a living. Losses of all kinds are grieving us. Comfort us in our grief. Be thou the lifter up of heads that causes us to say, "Lift up your hearts and praise God." We pray to you with confession of our sins. They are many. Many of them we know about and many of them we somehow don't know about. Help us by laboring together with us to overcome these sins. Purify us by your grace. Enter into the inner conversations of our hearts and say something significant to us that we will know are your words. We abide in you and rest in you in this hour. In the name of Jesus. Amen.

Prayer at the end of a sermon in St. Matthews Baptist Church
O Lord, our God and Jesus Christ our Lord, grant us as older persons to use our love to bless little children; to use our wisdom to have creative fellowship with the young. Grant us grace to be good role models and mentors for young adults. Empower us as we struggle alongside each other as older people and endow us each day with a sense of mission in the service of our Lord Jesus Christ. Heal us with the joy of your presence. In the name of our Lord Jesus Christ we pray. Amen.

A pastoral prayer offered during World War II
Our Father, who hast created us in Christ Jesus for all good works and apart from whom we can do nothing, we confess unto thee our iniquity, selfishness, and hatreds—sins of all sorts that are consuming us and our nation, making of us brutes of force rather than apostles of love. We as individuals and as a nation have done perversely; we have sinned; we have done that which is evil in thy sight. And what we have received is a double of our sins. But grant unto us forgiveness, we pray; that we will sing aloud of thy praise, thou who redeemeth our lives from destruction. Forbid that we should rise in the pride of military victory and be cast down into humiliation of a spiritual defeat.

Lead us and our loved ones, our enemies and their loved ones, out of the muck and mire of this awful blight and nightmare of war. Make us so sick of it that we shall join in a common spirit of reconciliation and understanding nevermore to follow the path of greed, self-seeking, and nationalistic pride, but take up the ministry of reconciliation which thou hast committed unto us, always to be peacemakers and children of God.

Grant unto us, we pray, the grace to be evangelists of healing ministries. Empower us to bring light to ignorant and confused minds, warped by the foolish and vain philosophies of men. Give us the strength to administer the balm of medical care to the broken and bleeding bodies of wounded and dying men and women and food to starving thousands. Humble us with a full expression of thy likeness in ourselves that we may bring unifying power from thee to the spirits of shattered personalities. And out of the confusion of this day of crisis, danger, and suffering, use us to establish order, peace, and security for mankind as a race and men as individuals. Forbid that we should boast save in Jesus Christ, our Lord. Amen.

Pastoral prayer, August 5, 1990, St. Matthews Baptist Church, Louisville, Kentucky
We are gathered together here, O living God, as the family of the people who have covenanted to love one another and worship you. We adore you as the One who is supreme over all other loyalties in our lives. In all the changing and sufferings of our lives, you are the One who changes not. You are the One who is from everlasting to everlasting. We revel in your steadfast love for us.

We confess unto you our weaknesses, our temptations. We bring our burdens to you, heavy as they are. You have spoken to us in him who is your Son that we can take upon ourselves his cross, his burden, for his burden is easy and his yoke is light. We thank you for having stood by us as a church through the many difficulties through which we have come. You have stood by us, you have held us together, and we pray now for an inspiration, a new spirit moving among our people. In the gladness of the worship of you, may we find in each other a family of God in whose presence we rejoice. In the name of Jesus Christ our Lord we pray. Amen.

Pastoral prayer, August 16, 1992, St. Matthews Baptist Church, Louisville, Kentucky

You have said, O God, "Be still and know that I am God," and we are going to be still for a moment or two to know that you are God. You have said, O God, through your servant, the Apostle Paul, that you are the Father of our Lord Jesus Christ and the God of all mercy and comfort. We turn to you for that mercy and that comfort and give you thanks that it comes to us through our Lord Jesus Christ who loves us and gave himself for us.

We turn to you, O God, in intercession for these that we have named. Comfort them in their times of discouragement; bring a light of hope and meaning to their suffering; sustain their families and enable them by the community of faith that we have here.

Accept our thanks, O God, for the abundance of your providence. When we consider the many things and opportunities and privileges that we have as we sit here this morning, we are overwhelmed by your generosity. Help us to be good stewards of this that we may be ministers of your grace through the abundance of our gifts, of your gifts to us. We pray especially today for Dr. and Mrs. Tuck in the renewing times of their vacation. Will you guide them and sustain them and bring new encouragement and joy to them as they return to us?

We ask you, O God, to be our guide in our times of our discouragement, confusion, and temptations to lose hope and temptations to despair. We should never despair because we know that you are the God of hope, the hope that never disappoints because the love of you has been shed abroad in our hearts through the Lord Jesus Christ in whose name we pray. Amen.

On January 10, 1982, fire destroyed the church sanctuary, office spaces, and part of the educational building at St. Matthews Baptist Church, Louisville, Kentucky, where Wayne Oates was a member. Over 800 people met for worship in Alumni Chapel that same morning at the Southern Baptist Theological Seminary, where Dr. Wayne Oates delivered the following prayer.

O God our help in ages past. Our hope for years to come. Be thou our shelter from the stormy blast and our eternal home. We give thee our thanks, our Heavenly Father, for the gift of fire to keep us warm, even as the warmth radiates up from the floor of this building to keep us warm. We thank thee for the gift of fire that helps us prepare our foods so that they will be warm and edible and nourishing.

We thank thee for fire which is a symbol, a picture, of the power of thy Holy Spirit descending upon us in a pentecostal way, separating itself to the foreheads of each of us. In fire thou hast endowed us with the gift of understanding. Through the power of thy Spirit thou dost create on earth, in spite of sin, in spite of man's inhumanity to man. We humbly believe we are the body of Christ, the church against whom the gates of hell shall not prevail. Yet we thank thee our Father for the fear that fire strikes into our hearts when it is out of control. We give thee our thanks that bodily all of us are here, and no one has been sent to a burn unit. We thank thee for the firemen who risked their lives, who withstood more cold and exposure than any of us may ever do. We thank thee for their families who share them with us. May we never take the work of firemen, of policemen, of doctors and nurses and hospitals for granted.

We thank thee, our Father, that we are gathered together in this holy place. Our church is not a building. We the people of God where we come together are the church. As we come here because fire, out of control, has been meant to us for evil, thy Spirit and thy power to guide us in such a fellowship wilt fulfill thy intention that this tragic happening shall be unto us for good. May it cleanse our motives and sharpen the direction of our ministry. May it empower us to reach out to those people in this community who never have enough heat, who never have enough food, who never have enough medicine, who never have enough care. Make us instruments of that kind of caring, through Jesus Christ whose we are, whom we serve, and whom we adore. Amen.

Cadet prayer at West Point Academy
God, our Father, thou searcher of men's hearts, help us to draw near to thee in sincerity and truth. May our religion be filled with gladness and may our worship of thee be natural.

Strengthen and increase our admiration for honest dealing and clean thinking, and suffer not our hatred of hypocrisy and pretense ever to diminish. Encourage us in our endeavor to live above the common level of life.

Make us to choose the harder right instead of the easier wrong, and never to be content with a half truth when the whole can be won.

Endow us with courage that is born of loyalty to all that is noble and worthy, that scorns to compromise with vice and injustice and knows no fear when truth and right are in jeopardy.

Guard us against flippancy and irreverence in the sacred things of life. Grant us new ties of friendship and new opportunities of service. Kindle our hearts in fellowship with those of a cheerful countenance, and soften our hearts with sympathy for those who sorrow and suffer.

Help us to maintain the honor of the Corps untarnished and unsullied and to show forth in our lives the ideals of West Point in doing our duty to thee and to our country.

All of which we ask in the name of the Great Friend and Master of men. Amen.

NOTES

1. Wayne E. Oates, *Nurturing Silence in a Noisy Heart* (Garden City NY: Doubleday & Co., 1979) 83ff.

2. Wayne E. Oates, *Temptation: A Biblical and Psychological Approach* (Louisville: Westminster/John Knox Press, 1991) 101–102.

3. Wayne E. Oates, *The Bible in Pastoral Care* (Philadelphia: Westminster Press, 1953) 108.

4. Ibid., 108–11.

5. Wayne E. Oates, *Your Right to Rest* (Philadelphia: The Westminster Press, 1984) 83–91.

6. Wayne E. Oates, *The Christian Pastor*, 3rd ed., rev. (Philadelphia: The Westminster Press, 1982) 151–52.

7. Ibid., 205–207.

8. Wayne E. Oates, compiler, *Grace Enough: Timeless Words for Trying Times* (Macon GA: Smyth & Helwys Publishing Co., 1996).

9. The following thirty-four prayers are taken from the "Prayers by Wayne E. Oates" in his class "Pastoral Care in Human Crises" at the Southern Baptist Theological Seminary, Louisville KY, Fall 1983.

10. These prayers were at the end of the devotions written by Oates for *The Upper Room Disciplines 1998* for February 24, 1998, February 25, 1998, and February 26, 1998.

Other available titles from

#Connect
Reaching Youth Across the Digital Divide
Brian Foreman

Reaching our youth across the digital divide is a struggle for parents, ministers, and other adults who work with Generation Z—today's teenagers. *#Connect* leads readers into the technological landscape, encourages conversations with teenagers, and reminds us all to be the presence of Christ in every facet of our lives.   978-1-57312-693-9 120 pages/pb **$13.00**

Beginnings
A Reverend and a Rabbi Talk About the Stories of Genesis
Michael Smith and Rami Shapiro

Editor Aaron Herschel Shapiro declares that stories "must be retold—not just repeated, but reinvented, reimagined, and reexperienced" to remain vital in the world. Mike and Rami continue their conversations from the *Mount and Mountain* books, exploring the places where their traditions intersect and diverge, listening to each other as they respond to the stories of Genesis.   978-1-57312-772-1 202 pages/pb **$18.00**

Bugles in the Afternoon
Dealing with Discouragement and Disillusionment in Ministry
Judson Edwards

In *Bugles in the Afternoon*, Edwards writes, "My long experience in the church has convinced me that most ministers—both professional and lay—spend time under the juniper tree. Those ministers who have served more than ten years and not been depressed, discouraged, or disillusioned can hold their annual convention in a phone booth."

978-1-57312-865-0 148 pages/pb **$16.00**

A Christian's Guide to Islam
Michael D. McCullar

A Christian's Guide to Islam provides a brief but accurate guide to Muslim formation, history, structure, beliefs, practices, and goals. It explores to what degree the tenets of Islam have been misinterpreted, corrupted, or abused over the centuries.

978-1-57312-512-3 128 pages/pb **$16.00**

To order call 1-800-747-3016 or visit www.helwys.com

Choosing Gratitude
Learning to Love the Life You Have
James A. Autry

Autry reminds us that gratitude is a choice, a spiritual—not social—process. He suggests that if we cultivate gratitude as a way of being, we may not change the world and its ills, but we can change our response to the world. If we fill our lives with moments of gratitude, we will indeed love the life we have. 978-1-57312-614-4 144 pages/pb **$15.00**

Choosing Gratitude 365 Days a Year
Your Daily Guide to Grateful Living
James A. Autry and Sally J. Pederson

Filled with quotes, poems, and the inspired voices of both Pederson and Autry, in a society consumed by fears of not having "enough"—money, possessions, security, and so on—this book suggests that if we cultivate gratitude as a way of being, we may not change the world and its ills, but we can change our response to the world. 978-1-57312-689-2 210 pages/pb **$18.00**

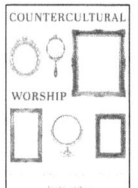
Countercultural Worship
A Plea to Evangelicals in a Secular Age
Mark G. McKim

Evangelical worship, McKim argues, has drifted far from both its biblical roots and historic origins, leaving evangelicals in danger of becoming mere chaplains to the wider culture, oblivious to the contradictions between what the secular culture says is real and important and what Scripture says is real and important. 978-1-57312-873-5 174 pages/pb **$19.00**

Crisis Ministry: A Handbook
Daniel G. Bagby

Covering more than 25 crisis pastoral care situations, this book provides a brief, practical guide for church leaders and other caregivers responding to stressful situations in the lives of parishioners. It tells how to resource caregiving professionals in the community who can help people in distress. 978-1-57312-370-9 154 pages/pb **$15.00**

Exemplars
Deacons as Servant and Spiritual Leaders
Elizabeth Allen and Daniel Vestal, eds.

Who Do Deacons Need to Be? What Do Deacons Need to Know? What Do Deacons Need to Do? These three questions form the basis for *Exemplars: Deacons as Servant and Spiritual Leaders*. They are designed to encourage robust conversation within diaconates as well as between deacons, clergy, and other laity. 978-1-57312-876-6 128 pages/pb **$15.00**

To order call 1-800-747-3016 or visit www.helwys.com

The Exile and Beyond (All the Bible series)
Wayne Ballard

The Exile and Beyond brings to life the sacred literature of Israel and Judah that comprises the exilic and postexilic communities of faith. It covers Ezekiel, Isaiah, Haggai, Zechariah, Malachi, 1 & 2 Chronicles, Ezra, Nehemiah, Joel, Jonah, Song of Songs, Esther, and Daniel. 978-1-57312-759-2 196 pages/pb **$16.00**

Fierce Love
Desperate Measures for Desperate Times
Jeanie Miley

Fierce Love is about learning to see yourself and know yourself as a conduit of love, operating from a full heart instead of trying to find someone to whom you can hook up your emotional hose and fill up your empty heart. 978-1-57312-810-0 276 pages/pb **$18.00**

Five Hundred Miles
Reflections on Calling and Pilgrimage
Lauren Brewer Bass

Spain's Camino de Santiago, the Way of St. James, has been a cherished pilgrimage path for centuries, visited by countless people searching for healing, solace, purpose, and hope. These stories from her five-hundred-mile-walk is Lauren Brewer Bass's honest look at the often winding, always surprising journey of a calling. 978-1-57312-812-4 142 pages/pb **$16.00**

A Five-Mile Walk
Exploring Themes in the Experience of Christian Faith and Discipleship
Michael B. Brown

Sometimes the Christian journey is a stroll along quiet shores. Other times it is an uphill climb on narrow, snow-covered mountain paths. Usually, it is simply walking in the direction of wholeness, one step after another, sometimes even two steps forward and one step back.
978-1-57312-852-0 196 pages/pb **$18.00**

Galatians (Smyth & Helwys Bible Commentary)
Marion L. Soards and Darrell J. Pursiful

In Galatians, Paul endeavored to prevent the Gentile converts from embracing a version of the gospel that insisted on their observance of a form of the Mosaic Law. He saw with a unique clarity that such a message reduced the crucified Christ to being a mere agent of the Law. For Paul, the gospel of Jesus Christ alone, and him crucified, had no place in it for the claim that Law-observance was necessary for believers to experience the power of God's grace. 978-1-57312-771-4 384 pages/hc **$55.00**

To order call **1-800-747-3016** or visit **www.helwys.com**

Glimpses from State Street
Wayne Ballard

As a collection of devotionals, *Glimpses from State Street* provides a wealth of insights and new ways to consider and develop our fellowship with Christ. It also serves as a window into the relationship between a small town pastor and a welcoming congregation.

978-1-57312-841-4 158 pages/pb **$15.00**

God's Servants, the Prophets
Bryan Bibb

God's Servants, the Prophets covers the Israelite and Judean prophetic literature from the preexilic period. It includes Amos, Hosea, Isaiah, Micah, Zephaniah, Nahum, Habakkuk, Jeremiah, and Obadiah.

978-1-57312-758-5 208 pages/pb **$16.00**

Gray Matters
100 Devotions for the Aging
Edwin Ray Frazier

"Each line rests on Frazier's fundamental belief that every season in life is valuable and rich with opportunity."

—Alicia Davis Porterfield
Interim pastor and former eldercare chaplain

978-1-57312-837-7 246 pages/pb **$18.00**

Hermeneutics of Hymnody
A Comprehensive and Integrated Approach to Understanding Hymns
Scotty Gray

Scotty Gray's *Hermeneutics of Hymnody* is a comprehensive and integrated approach to understanding hymns. It is unique in its holistic and interrelated exploration of seven of the broad facets of this most basic forms of Christian literature. A chapter is devoted to each and relates that facet to all of the others.

978-157312-767-7 432 pages/pb **$28.00**

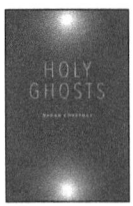
Holy Ghosts
Ragan Courtney

"When the dead come to mind, they are like holy ghosts, as real as hope or faith, as tangible as trust and love. This book is a collection of questions, memories, and loves that continue to live with me, in me, and through me. . . . Here is displayed the basis of my personal faith that encompasses the story of a man who rose from the dead and showed all who would see that death is not the end. Life is. Period."—Preface

978-157312-871-1 124 pages/pb **$6.00**

To order call 1-800-747-3016 or visit www.helwys.com

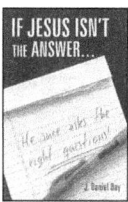
If Jesus Isn't the Answer . . . He Sure Asks the Right Questions!
J. Daniel Day

Taking eleven of Jesus' questions as its core, Day invites readers into their own conversation with Jesus. Equal parts testimony, theological instruction, pastoral counseling, and autobiography, the book is ultimately an invitation to honest Christian discipleship.

978-1-57312-797-4 148 pages/pb **$16.00**

James M. Dunn and Soul Freedom
Aaron Douglas Weaver

James Milton Dunn, over the last fifty years, has been the most aggressive Baptist proponent for religious liberty in the US. Soul freedom—voluntary, uncoerced faith and an unfettered individual conscience before God—is the basis of his understanding of church-state separation and the historic Baptist basis of religious liberty.

978-1-57312-590-1 224 pages/pb **$18.00**

Judaism
A Brief Guide to Faith and Practice
Sharon Pace

Sharon Pace's newest book is a sensitive and comprehensive introduction to Judaism. How does belief in the One God and a universal morality shape the way in which Jews see the world? How does one find meaning in life and the courage to endure suffering? How does one mark joy and forge community ties?

978-1-57312-644-1 144 pages/pb **$16.00**

Loyal Dissenters
Reading Scripture and Talking Freedom with 17th-century English Baptists
Lee Canipe

When Baptists in 17th-century England wanted to talk about freedom, they unfailingly began by reading the Bible—and what they found in Scripture inspired their compelling (and, ultimately, successful) arguments for religious liberty. In an age of widespread anxiety, suspicion, and hostility, these early Baptists refused to worship God in keeping with the king's command.

978-1-57312-872-8 178 pages/pb **$19.00**

To order call **1-800-747-3016** or visit **www.helwys.com**

Luke (Smyth & Helwys Annual Bible Study series)
Parables for the Journey
Michael L. Ruffin

These stories in Luke's Gospel are pilgrimage parables. They are parables for those on the way to being the people of God. They are not places where we stop and stay; they are rather places where we learn what we need to learn and from which, equipped with Jesus' directions, we continue the journey. But we will see that they are also places to which we repeatedly return.

Teaching Guide 978-1-57312-849-0 146 pages/pb **$14.00**
Study Guide 978-1-57312-850-6 108 pages/pb **$6.00**

Meditations on Mark
Daily Devotions from the Oldest Gospel
Chris Cadenhead

Readers searching for a fresh encounter with Scripture can delve into *Meditations on Mark*, a collection of daily devotions intended to guide the reader through the book of Mark, the Oldest Gospel and the first known effort to summarize and proclaim the life and ministry of Jesus.

978-1-57312-851-3 158 pages/pb **$15.00**

Meeting Jesus Today
For the Cautious, the Curious, and the Committed
Jeanie Miley

Meeting Jesus Today, ideal for both individual study and small groups, is intended to be used as a workbook. It is designed to move readers from studying the Scriptures and ideas within the chapters to recording their journey with the Living Christ.

978-1-57312-677-9 320 pages/pb **$19.00**

Of Mice and Ministers
Musings and Conversations About Life, Death, Grace, and Everything
Bert Montgomery

With stories about pains, joys, and everyday life, *Of Mice and Ministers* finds Jesus in some unlikely places and challenges us to do the same. From tattooed women ministers to saying the "N"-word to the brotherly kiss, Bert Montgomery takes seriously the lesson from Psalm 139—where can one go that God is not already there?

978-1-57312-733-2 154 pages/pb **$14.00**

To order call **1-800-747-3016** or visit **www.helwys.com**

Place Value
The Journey to Where You Are
Katie Sciba

Does a place have value? Can a place change us? Is it possible for God to use the place you are in to form you? From Victoria, Texas to Indonesia, Belize, Australia, and beyond, Katie Sciba's wanderlust serves as a framework to understand your own places of deep emotion and how God may have been weaving redemption around you all along.

978-157312-829-2 138 pages/pb **$15.00**

Preaching that Connects
Charles B. Bugg and Alan Redditt

How does the minister stay focused on the holy when the daily demands of the church seem relentless? How do we come to a preaching event with a sense that God is working in us and through us? In *Preaching that Connects*, Charles Bugg and Alan Redditt explore the balancing act of a minister's authority as preacher, sharing what the congregation needs to hear, and the communal role as pastor, listening to God alongside congregants.

978-157312-887-2 128 pages/pb **$15.00**

Reading Joshua
(Reading the Old Testament series)
A Historical-Critical/Archaeological Commentary
John C. H. Laughlin

Using the best of current historical-critical studies by mainstream biblical scholars, and the most recent archaeological discoveries and theorizing, Laughlin questions both the historicity of the stories presented in the book as well as the basic theological ideology presented through these stories: namely that Yahweh ordered the indiscriminate butchery of the Canaanites.

978-1-57312-836-0 274 pages/pb **$32.00**

Reading Nahum–Malachi
(Reading the Old Testament series)
A Literary and Theological Commentary
Steven Tuell

This commentary maintains a balance between reading each of these six books in its own historical and social setting and considering the interrelationships and canonical functions of these books within the Book of the Twelve as a whole. Jesus ben Sirach wrote that "the Twelve Prophets . . . comforted the people of Jacob and delivered them with confident hope" (Sir 49:10). This commentary, following ben Sirach, proposes that the theme of the Book of the Twelve is a comforting word of hope and deliverance.

978-1-57312-838-3 304 pages/pb **$33.00**

To order call **1-800-747-3016** or visit **www.helwys.com**

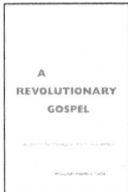

A Revolutionary Gospel
Salvation in the Theology of Walter Rauschenbusch
William Powell Tuck

William Powell Tuck describes how Rauschenbusch's concept of redemption requires a transformation of society as well as individuals—and that no one can genuinely be redeemed without this redemption affecting the social culture as well. *A Revolutionary Gospel* shows us how Rauschenbusch's revolutionary concept of salvation is still relevant today.

978-1-57312-804-9 190 pages/pb **$21.00**

Sessions with Ezra & Nehemiah (Sessions Bible Studies series)
New Beginnings with God
Randy Shepley

Ezra and Nehemiah address questions that continue to be relevant for believers today: How does a religious group embody their faith as a minority movement in a larger, pluralistic culture? How do church leaders guide people of faith to develop courage and holiness? Ezra and Nehemiah also provide encouragement to churches who struggle with the nostalgia of their past even as they move forward into their future, as well as those moving from disordered chaos to spiritual community.

978-1-57312-866-7 128 pages/pb **$13.00**

Sessions with Psalms (Sessions Bible Studies series)
Prayers for All Seasons
Eric and Alicia D. Porterfield

Useful to seminar leaders during preparation and group discussion, as well as in individual Bible study, *Sessions with Psalms* is a ten-session study designed to explore what it looks like for the words of the psalms to become the words of our prayers. Each session is followed by a thought-provoking page of questions.

978-1-57312-768-4 136 pages/pb **$14.00**

Star Thrower
A Pastor's Handbook
William Powell Tuck

In his latest book, *Star Thrower: A Pastor's Handbook*, William Powell Tuck draws on over fifty years of experience to share his perspective on being an effective pastor. He describes techniques for sermon preparation, pastoral care, and church administration, as well as for conducting Communion, funeral, wedding, and baptismal services. He also includes advice for working with laity and church staff, coping with church conflict, and nurturing one's own spiritual and family life.

978-1-57312-889-6 244 pages/pb **$15.00**

To order call 1-800-747-3016 or visit www.helwys.com

Tell the Truth, Shame the Devil
Stories about the Challenges of Young Pastors
James Elllis III, ed.

A pastor's life is uniquely difficult. *Tell the Truth, Shame the Devil*, then, is an attempt to expose some of the challenges that young clergy often face. While not exhaustive, this collection of essays is a superbly compelling and diverse introduction to how tough being a pastor under the age of thirty-five can be. 978-1-57312-839-1 198 pages/pb **$18.00**

Though the Darkness Gather Round
Devotions about Infertility, Miscarriage, and Infant Loss
Mary Elizabeth Hill Hanchey and Erin McClain, eds.

Much courage is required to weather the long grief of infertility and the sudden grief of miscarriage and infant loss. This collection of devotions by men and women, ministers, chaplains, and lay leaders who can speak of such sorrow, is a much-needed resource and precious gift for families on this journey and the faith communities that walk beside them.

978-1-57312-811-7 180 pages/pb **$19.00**

Time for Supper
Invitations to Christ's Table
Brett Younger

Some scholars suggest that every meal in literature is a communion scene. Could every meal in the Bible be a communion text? Could every passage be an invitation to God's grace? These meditations on the Lord's Supper help us listen to the myriad of ways God invites us to gratefully, reverently, and joyfully share the cup of Christ. 978-1-57312-720-2 246 pages/pb **$18.00**

A True Hope
Jedi Perils and the Way of Jesus
Joshua Hays

Star Wars offers an accessible starting point for considering substantive issues of faith, philosophy, and ethics. In *A True Hope*, Joshua Hays explores some of these challenging ideas through the sayings of the Jedi Masters, examining the ways the worldview of the Jedi is at odds with that of the Bible. 978-1-57312-770-7 186 pages/pb **$18.00**

To order call **1-800-747-3016** or visit **www.helwys.com**

Clarence Jordan's Cotton Patch Gospel

The Complete Collection

Hardback • 448 pages
Retail 50.00 • Your Price 25.00

Paperback • 448 pages
Retail 40.00 • Your Price 20.00

The Cotton Patch Gospel, by Koinonia Farm founder Clarence Jordan, recasts the stories of Jesus and the letters of the New Testament into the language and culture of the mid-twentieth-century South. Born out of the civil rights struggle, these now-classic translations of much of the New Testament bring the far-away places of Scripture closer to home: Gainesville, Selma, Birmingham, Atlanta, Washington D.C.

More than a translation, *The Cotton Patch Gospel* continues to make clear the startling relevance of Scripture for today. Now for the first time collected in a single, hardcover volume, this edition comes complete with a new Introduction by President Jimmy Carter, a Foreword by Will D. Campbell, and an Afterword by Tony Campolo. Smyth & Helwys Publishing is proud to help reintroduce these seminal works of Clarence Jordan to a new generation of believers, in an edition that can be passed down to generations still to come.

To order call **1-800-747-3016**
or visit **www.helwys.com**

www.ingramcontent.com/pod-product-compliance
Lightning Source LLC
Chambersburg PA
CBHW062109080426
42734CB00012B/2806